Lionel Messi

Sebastian Gomez

GRAPEVINE INDIA

Published by

GRAPEVINE INDIA PUBLISHERS PVT LTD

www.grapevineindia.com
Delhi | Mumbai
email: grapevineindiapublishers@gmail.com

Ordering Information:
Quantity sales: Special discounts are available on quantity
purchases by corporations, associations, and others.
For details, reach out to the publisher.

First published by Grapevine India 2025

CONTENTS

TIMELINE

Year	Event
2000	Moved to Barcelona at age 13 and joined La Masia academy.
2001	Began hormone treatment for growth deficiency, funded by Barcelona.
Nov 16, 2003	Made first-team debut for Barcelona in a friendly against FC Porto at 16.
Oct 16, 2004	Official La Liga debut for Barcelona vs. Espanyol.
May 1, 2005	Scored first goal for Barcelona's senior team against Albacete, assisted by Ronaldinho.
June 2005	Won FIFA U-20 World Cup with Argentina, scoring two goals in the final.
Aug 17, 2005	Made senior Argentina debut vs. Hungary but was sent off after 43 seconds.
Sep 2005	Signed first professional contract with Barcelona.
Nov 2005	Became a regular starter for Barcelona under Frank Rijkaard.
May 17, 2006	Won first UEFA Champions League title with Barcelona, though he missed the final due to injury.
Mar 10, 2007	Scored his first hat-trick for Barcelona in El Clásico vs. Real Madrid (3-3).
Apr 18, 2007	Scored Maradona-like solo goal against Getafe, dribbling from his own half.
Dec 2007	Finished third in the Ballon d'Or voting for the first time.
Aug 23, 2008	Won Olympic gold with Argentina in Beijing.
Dec 2008	Finished second in the Ballon d'Or, behind Cristiano Ronaldo.

Year	Event
May 27, 2009	Scored in the Champions League final vs. Manchester United, helping Barcelona win the treble.
Dec 1, 2009	Won his first Ballon d'Or, officially becoming the best player in the world.
Mar 10, 2010	Scored four goals in a single UCL match vs. Arsenal, his first such feat.
May 2010	Won second La Liga title in a row with Barcelona, finishing as top scorer.
June-July 2010	Led Argentina at the 2010 World Cup, but was eliminated in the quarterfinals by Germany.
2011	Won Ballon d'Or for the third consecutive time. Scored in the Champions League final vs. Manchester United, winning the title.
2012	Set a world record for most goals in a calendar year (91 goals). Won fourth Ballon d'Or.
2013	Suffered multiple injuries, missing crucial games. Finished second in Ballon d'Or voting behind Cristiano Ronaldo.
2014	Led Argentina to the FIFA World Cup final, winning the Golden Ball as the tournament's best player. Became La Liga's all-time top scorer.
2015	Won second treble with Barcelona (La Liga, Copa del Rey, UCL). Won his fifth Ballon d'Or.
2016	Announced international retirement after losing the Copa América final but reversed his decision. Barcelona won La Liga and Copa del Rey.
2017	Scored a last-minute winner in El Clásico at the Bernabéu. Neymar left for PSG, ending the MSN trio.

Year	Event
2018	Became Barcelona captain after Iniesta's departure. Barcelona won La Liga, but Messi suffered a shock UCL exit vs. Roma.
2019	Won sixth Ballon d'Or, surpassing Ronaldo. Barcelona suffered a 4-0 UCL collapse vs. Liverpool.
2020	Barcelona suffered an 8-2 loss to Bayern Munich in UCL. Messi sent a burofax requesting to leave but was forced to stay.
2021	Left Barcelona due to financial issues. Signed with Paris Saint-Germain (PSG). Won Copa América with Argentina, his first major international title.
2022	Won FIFA World Cup with Argentina, scoring twice in the final. Won seventh Ballon d'Or.
2023	Left PSG and joined Inter Miami in MLS. Won Leagues Cup, his first trophy in the U.S. Won eighth Ballon d'Or.
2024	Continues to break records in MLS and prepares for Copa América 2024.

INTRODUCTION

Lionel Messi stood on the precipice of footballing immortality, knowing that one final triumph would complete his unparalleled legacy.

At Lusail Stadium, under the bright Qatari lights, Argentina's greatest son finally seized the moment he had chased for nearly two decades. The World Cup was his at last, but not without a final battle that tested every ounce of his resilience, brilliance, and will to win.

From the first whistle, Messi was in control of the outcome. He opened the scoring with an ice-cold penalty, sending Hugo Lloris the wrong way and writing his name into history as the first player to score in every knockout round of a single World Cup. He wasn't finished. Moments later, in a move of pure artistry, he orchestrated a stunning counterattack that led to Ángel Di María's goal. Argentina were in complete control, playing with the kind of confidence that suggested this would be a coronation, not a contest.

But football, like fate, is never straightforward. Kylian Mbappé, the heir to Messi's throne, refused to let history be written without him. In a span of 97 seconds, the French prodigy shattered Argentina's dominance, first converting a penalty before unleashing a breathtaking volley that sent the match into chaos. Messi's moment of destiny was slipping away, his disbelief etched across the giant screens in the stadium. It was happening again.

Extra time arrived, and once more, Messi willed Argentina forward. In the 108th minute, he found himself in the perfect spot, bundling in a rebound to put Argentina ahead once more. The stadium exploded—surely, this time, it was over. But fate, and Mbappé, had other plans. Another penalty, another equalizer. It was a game for the ages, refusing to grant Messi his moment without one final test.

And so it came to penalties. As Argentina's Emiliano Martínez denied France, Messi, ever the calm architect, converted his own with surgical precision. Finally, when Gonzalo Montiel slotted home the winning spot-kick, the weight of decades lifted. The World Cup, the missing piece, belonged to Messi. As he lifted the trophy in his hands, draped in the regal bisht, there was no more debate, no more waiting—only glory.

Lionel Messi is considered a legendary footballer not just for his statistics, but for the way he redefined the sport with his skill, vision, and longevity. His career is a story of brilliance, resilience, and an insatiable hunger for success. From the streets of Rosario to the grandest stages of world football, Messi's journey has been nothing short of extraordinary.

What sets Messi apart is his ability to dominate the game for nearly two decades. Winning eight Ballon d'Ors, four Champions League titles, and 10 La Liga crowns, he became Barcelona's all-time top scorer and the highest scorer in La Liga history. His dribbling, close control, and unmatched ability to change the course of a game made him a nightmare for defenders. But beyond the numbers, it was the artistry—the effortless turns, the inch-perfect passes, and the dazzling solo runs—that left fans and opponents in awe.

For years, critics pointed to the absence of a major international title as the only missing piece in Messi's legacy. He answered them emphatically.

In 2021, he guided Argentina to Copa América glory, lifting his first senior international trophy. Then, in 2022, he cemented his place in football history by delivering Argentina their third World Cup title in one of the greatest finals of all time. Scoring twice in the final and converting in the penalty shootout, he became the first player to score in every round of a World Cup. The sheer drama of the night at Lusail Stadium, where Messi fought against the brilliance of Kylian Mbappé, only added to his legend.

Yet, what makes Messi truly iconic is his consistency over time. Few players sustain excellence for more than a few seasons; Messi has done it for nearly two decades. Whether at Barcelona, Paris Saint-Germain, or now Inter Miami, he continues to mesmerize. His story is one of relentless pursuit—of records, of trophies, and of perfection. More than just a footballer, Messi is an artist, a magician, and for many, the greatest to ever play the game.

Writing this biography of Lionel Messi was a journey that took countless hours of research, reading, and analysis. I pored over interviews, watched documentaries, and sifted through old match reports, tracing every step of his evolution from a boy in Rosario to the global icon he is today. I read firsthand accounts from coaches, teammates, and even rivals, trying to understand what made Messi different—not just as a player but as a person. His story has been told in many ways, but I wanted to capture the depth of his journey, the sacrifices that shaped him, and the relentless drive that made him the greatest.

What first drew me to Messi was his background. Unlike many football legends who grew up in football academies, groomed from the start for greatness, Messi came from a working-class family in Argentina. His story wasn't just about talent; it was about resilience, sacrifice, and adaptation. Moving to Barcelona at 13, leaving behind his home and his loved ones, undergoing painful hormone treatments to fight his growth deficiency—these were struggles that made his rise even more extraordinary. His family uprooted their lives so he could chase his dream, and in doing so, he carried not just his own hopes but theirs as well.

As a biographer, my work didn't stop at reading interviews or watching highlights. I analyzed his playing style, compared accounts of different periods in his career, and examined the psychological toll of his defeats as much as the euphoria of his triumphs. Understanding Messi required understanding his failures—how he responded to heartbreak in the 2014 World Cup, how he handled the pressure of carrying Argentina, and how he nearly walked away from international football altogether.

I also delved into the Messi that exists off the pitch. His loyalty, his reserved nature, his deep bond with his family—these elements helped me paint a fuller picture of the man behind the number 10 jersey.

What emerged was a portrait of someone who never sought the spotlight but was thrust into it by sheer brilliance. Writing this biography became more than just a bland chronicle of football history. It was a unique story of sacrifice, perseverance, and the unwavering pursuit of greatness.

CHAPTER 1
A BOY FROM ROSARIO

The Birthplace of a Legend

The streets of Argentina pulsed with unrest, the echoes of war still fresh. Five years after the Falklands War, the military junta had collapsed, but chaos remained. Economic turmoil and public outrage fueled protests, while rogue factions threatened civil conflict. As democracy struggled to take hold, citizens filled the streets, demanding justice and a future free from tyranny.

It was in this climate of uncertainty, that Lionel Andrés Messi was born.

In the early hours of June 24, 1987, a woman was rushed through the doors of Garibaldi Hospital in Rosario. The cream-colored walls of the 19th-century building, dedicated to the Italian revolutionary hero Giuseppe Garibaldi, had seen countless births—but this one would be different.

Inside, Celia Cuccittini fought through the pain, her contractions coming faster now. Outside, the world teetered on the edge of chaos. Her husband, Jorge, gripped her hand, his face lined with worry.

Complications arose. The doctor, sensing distress, considered intervention. Jorge, standing beside Celia, pleaded with him to avoid using forceps, terrified of the risks. The minutes stretched, thick with tension, until at last, a cry pierced the air. At exactly 6:00 AM, a small, red-faced baby, his ear folded from the strain of birth, blinked into the dim hospital light. The fear in the room melted into quiet joy.

His parents, Jorge and Celia, grew up just a few steps from each other in Rosario's working-class neighborhood. Their families, descendants of Italian and Spanish immigrants, had settled in the city, carrying with them traditions, resilience, and a deep sense of community. Jorge's father, Eusebio, worked in construction, while Celia's father repaired appliances. Their shared world, woven together by humble beginnings and hard work, set the foundation for their love.

Jorge and Celia married young. Argentina was in the grip of World Cup fever, and even on their honeymoon, the newlyweds made time to watch Argentina play Brazil. A week later, the country erupted in celebration as Argentina won the World Cup. The moment of triumph overshadowed the brutal military dictatorship that controlled the nation. Amidst the uncertainty of the era, Jorge and Celia started their own family.

Their first son, Rodrigo Martín, was born on February 9, 1980, bringing joy to a household that stood resilient despite the economic turmoil and political unrest in Argentina. Two years later, their son Matías was born on June 25, 1982, just days after Argentina's devastating loss in the Falklands War. The military junta, already weakened by its failed invasion, would soon collapse, marking the return of democracy. Yet, the wounds of war and dictatorship remained fresh, shaping the world into which the Messi boys were born.

Argentina was still grappling with political instability, a nation on edge, its future uncertain. But inside that hospital, in the arms of his exhausted mother, a new kind of hope had arrived. The child who would grow up to mesmerize the world with his genius had taken his first breath.

A Toddler's First Steps Toward Football

At six months, Lionel Messi appeared chubby and smiling in family albums, dressed in blue trousers and a white t-shirt. By ten months, he was chasing after his older brothers, but he had his first accident rather quickly. A bicycle knocked him down outside their home. Though the initial shock subsided, his swollen arm revealed a broken ulna, requiring a cast.

On his first birthday, relatives had gifted him a Newell's Old Boys jersey, but at three, he preferred marbles, collecting them in bags won from playmates. For his fourth birthday, his parents gave him a white ball with red diamonds. One day, he abandoned his marbles to join his father and brothers in a street game. "We were stunned when we saw what he could do," Jorge had recalled. It was his first touch of destiny.

Jorge Messi, like his father Eusebio, was a builder, and together they spent weekends expanding their modest family home in Rosario's working-class neighborhood. It was a small, single-story house with a backyard for playing and a wall facing the home of Leo's childhood best friend.

Over time, the house changed—a second floor, a security fence, a camera—but in the early years, it was simple. "Small," Leo recalled. "A kitchen, living room, two bedrooms. My parents in one, me and my brothers in the other."

Just 200 meters away, a rough, fenced-off field was where local kids played football. Nearby was the kiosk where Matías worked long after Leo had left for Barcelona, and Grandoli, the club where Leo first kicked a ball. His grandmother Celia lived close by, as did his cousins. Further up the street, his grandparents remained rooted in their family home, where even at 86, his grandfather still opened his small bakery each morning.

Family was everything. Leo's devotion to his family was unwavering. He had a tattoo of his mother's face on his back, a surprise even to them. "He came home one day and showed us," Jorge recalled. "We almost fainted."

More than wealth or fame, Leo cherished home—Rosario, La Bajada—the place he never truly left. Whenever possible, he returned, escaping to his roots. Though now living in a larger home outside the city, he was still seen cycling through the neighborhood or shopping in small-town supermarkets, always recognized, never hiding behind security.

The Beginning of a Dream

In early 1994, Lionel Messi arrived at Newell's Old Boys, already a player to watch. Club scouts had heard of his talent and invited his brothers to bring him along. Over a month, he played eight games in different formations, proving himself at every turn. The Newell's coaches were astonished and quickly recommended him for the Escuela de Fútbol Malvinas, a program designed for the youngest footballing talents. He was not even seven years old.

Jorge had no doubts. "I'm going to take him to Newell's," he told Leo's coach, who simply shrugged—what else could he say? On March 21, 1994, Lionel Andrés Messi, ID number 992312, officially became a Newell's Old Boys player.

Newell's, founded in 1903, was one of Rosario's two great football clubs, its fierce rivalry with Rosario Central dividing the city's football loyalties. Founded by British railway workers, Rosario Central boasted football legends and even counted Che Guevara among its famous supporters. Newell's, by contrast, had an English influence of its own—founded by teachers and students of the Argentine Commercial Anglican School, named after its Kent-born founder, Isaac Newell. The club's black and red colors honored the school's traditions.

Six years before Lionel Messi's name would first appear in La Capital, Rosario's local newspaper, he was already carving out his legend at Newell's Old Boys. The faded murals and rusted fences of the Escuela de Fútbol Malvinas were a stark contrast to the raw talent developing within. While the facilities lacked investment, enthusiasm burned brightly among the young players. Messi's first season in Newell's red and black ended in disappointment—a 3-0 defeat that cost them the title.

But the boys learned from it. Over the next four seasons, they would lose just once, forming the legendary Máquina del '87—the '87 Machine.

One of Messi's greatest early triumphs came in 1996 at the Cantolao tournament in Lima, Peru. Competing against teams from Argentina, Chile, Ecuador, and Colombia, Newell's emerged victorious, and Messi stood out. His dribbling and ball control mesmerized spectators, so much so that the club's directors invited him to entertain crowds at halftime during first-team matches. Announced over the stadium speakers, the tiny boy with a ball at his feet became a spectacle, dazzling fans with his keepy-uppy tricks.

Messi's coach saw something special in him. "He didn't need to be taught. What can you teach to a Maradona or a Pelé?" he recalled. In one unforgettable moment, Messi picked up the ball in defense, ran the entire length of the pitch, and scored an astonishing solo goal. His talent was undeniable, and his teammates knew it. Th defender summed it up best: "Once Messi had the ball, the opposition just got out of the way."

In 2000, Lionel Messi played his final season with the Máquina del '87, guiding the team to victory in the tenth league. The triumph at Bella Vista, the training ground of Newell's first team, marked the end of an era. Just weeks later, on September 3, La Capital published his first-ever interview—a double-page spread titled "Lionel Andrés Messi, a Little Leper Who's a Real Handful."

The article described a boy with extraordinary skill, capable of weaving past defenders effortlessly, scoring goals, but most importantly, playing with joy. His answers in the interview revealed his deep-rooted love for family and football. His idols? His father and godfather. His favorite players? His brother and cousin. His dream? To play for Newell's first team.

Even then, his humility shone through. "Humility is something a human being should never lose," he said. His happiest moment was winning the tenth league; his saddest, the loss of his grandmother—the woman who first took him to play football.

Despite his impending departure for Barcelona, his heart remained with Newell's. "What does Newell's mean to you?" they asked. His answer was simple: "Everything. The best."

The Making of a Champion

Every Sunday, without fail, Leo Messi would arrive at his grandmother Celia's house, where the narrow concrete patch in front became his first playing field. With his brothers, Rodrigo and Matías, and later his cousins Maxi and Emanuel, the games began—rondos, foot tennis, or just football with two rocks for goalposts. First to six goals. The rules were simple; the competition, fierce.

Inside, the women of the family—Celia, her daughters Celia and Marcela—prepared pasta, the rich aroma filling the small house. The men, Jorge and Claudio, sat in the living room, half-watching the game, half-arguing about football. "Good, Maxi, good!" Jorge shouted, a former Newell's Old Boys player himself. Every kick, every dribble, was met with pride, especially when it came to Leo. "Look at him, as small as he is—impossible to take the ball from him," someone would murmur.

The call for dinner broke the game, but only briefly. Hands were washed, plates were filled, yet no one wanted to be away from the ball for long. The cousins ate quickly, already clutching the football under their arms, eager to return to the square nearby. There, the games resumed, sometimes for hours.

The matches weren't always fair. The older boys—Rodrigo, Matías, and Maxi—took on the younger ones, Leo and Emanuel. The tackles were rougher, the play faster. Leo, small but determined, bore the brunt of the kicks. "Matías, careful, man!" Jorge would warn. But Leo never backed down. He chased the ball relentlessly, and once he had it, he refused to let go. His uncle Claudio remembers him red-faced, veins bulging, unwilling to accept defeat.

And if he lost? There would be tears, anger, a tantrum no one could console.

"Always ended badly," Leo later admitted in an interview, "even if we won, my brother would annoy me just to make me mad."

Some games drew in neighbors, teams formed from rival streets. The Messi/Cuccittini team never lost. Matías recalled, "At first, they didn't want to play against us—Leo was too small. Then, after the game, they congratulated him. He was nine, playing against guys nearly twice his age, and they couldn't stop him."

It was no surprise that footballers emerged from this family. Rodrigo played for Newell's younger division before a car accident ended his career. "He was very good," Leo later said, "but in those days, an injury like that meant the end." Matías, a defender, played for Newell's lower ranks before stepping away, only to return years later, playing until 27.

Maximiliano, at just 1.65 meters, built a career across Argentina, Paraguay, Mexico, and Brazil. His resilience showed when, after fracturing his skull in training, he fought his way back. The night his daughter was born prematurely, he scored for Flamengo, while in Spain, Leo hit a hat trick for Barcelona and dedicated the goals to her.

At 13, Leo left for Barcelona. The Sunday meals, the fierce games in the square, became memories. The cousins grew up, their lives taking separate paths. But some part of those childhood games stayed with them, just as they stayed with Leo. The little boy who never wanted to lose had taken that fire with him to Spain.

When Leo was ten, Celia, his beloved grandmother, passed away. She had been more than just a grandmother—she was his greatest believer. The boy who played for hours outside her house carried her memory with him, whispering her name every time he scored.

CHAPTER 2
THE GROWTH HORMONE BATTLE

A Life-Changing Diagnosis

On January 31, 1997, Doctor Diego met a nine-year-old Lionel Messi for the first time.

Concerned about their son's small stature, Jorge and Celia had taken him to the Clinic for Glands and Internal Medicine in Rosario. At just 1.27 meters tall, Messi was significantly smaller than his peers.

The doctor conducted months of tests, ruling out natural late development before diagnosing a rare growth hormone deficiency. "His glands weren't making any growth hormone," Doctor Diego explained. "It's like diabetes—just as a diabetic's pancreas doesn't produce insulin, Lionel's body wasn't producing what he needed to grow."

The condition was extremely rare, affecting only one in 20 million people. It wasn't hereditary—his siblings, including his younger sister María Sol, were all of normal height.

Despite the daunting diagnosis, Messi handled the situation with remarkable resilience. "He had a healthy relationship with his illness," Doctor Diego recalled. "Even the most invasive tests never seemed to shake him. His family was first-class in their support."

The treatment required daily subcutaneous injections of growth hormone, continuing for at least three to six years. Progress was monitored through hand x-rays, which showed open spaces between bones that would eventually close as growth completed. "Nothing can override genetics," the doctor explained, "but if the body lacks something essential, we can intervene."

Some later speculated that Messi was part of an experimental procedure, a notion Doctor Diego dismissed angrily. "It was never an experiment," he insisted. Growth hormone therapy had been used for decades. Originally extracted from cadavers—until risks of Creutzfeldt-Jakob disease were discovered—it had been safely produced through genetic engineering since the 1980s. "Messi's treatment was medically necessary," he emphasized.

However, the use of growth hormones remained controversial, particularly in sports. Administered to healthy adults, it functioned as an anabolic steroid, increasing muscle mass and reducing fat. But the health risks were serious, ranging from water retention to hyperthyroidism, high blood sugar, and even cranial hypertension.

Lionel Messi's growth hormone treatment was a crucial yet costly necessity, amounting to 600,000 Argentine pesos per year—roughly £100,000. While some in Argentina believed the treatment could have been covered domestically, the Messi family saw their financial support gradually slip away.

Initially, Jorge's social security and the Acindar Foundation helped cover the expenses. Later, Newell's Old Boys stepped in to pay for half of the injections, recognizing Messi's talent. However, their payments became inconsistent. "We went so many times to ask for the money," Jorge recalled. "In the end, my wife said, 'I'm not going to ask anymore.'"

Desperate for a solution, the Messis turned to the club River Plate, where Messi impressed during trials. The club wanted him, but only if they could secure his release from Newell's. That never happened. Newell's, reluctant to lose their star prospect, made more promises, but the money never came.

Then came Barcelona.

A Journey to Barcelona

On October 2, 2000, Barcelona's technical director Charly watched a boy weave through defenders as if they were standing still. "Who's that?" he asked, though he already knew the answer. "Messi," came the reply.

"We've got to sign him—now!"

At thirteen, Lionel Messi was already a standout in Argentina's youth football scene. Newspapers wrote about his performances, and clubs like River Plate took notice. Yet despite the attention, no concrete offers came, and financial concerns over his growth hormone treatment remained unresolved.

The Messi family had been cautious about agents making empty promises, but in 2000, two player representatives approached them, claiming they could secure Lionel a European trial. Jorge Messi remained skeptical, knowing that until a real opportunity arose, no one would cover the costs. But in August, a breakthrough came. Through contacts in Barcelona, Messi's name reached influential figures within the club.

Instead of sending scouts to Argentina, Barcelona invited Messi to Spain for a trial. It was a gamble, but it was the best way for the club to assess him. If all went well, Barcelona could become Messi's new home, offering both footballing promise and the financial security his family desperately needed.

While some viewed the move to Spain as purely a financial decision, Doctor Diego dismissed that notion. "The hormone deficiency is just an anecdote," he insisted. "What really matters is his footballing ability." Messi's talent was undeniable—his speed, ball control, and vision set him apart. Yet in Argentina, success often meant playing for a Buenos Aires club.

As Messi's treatment became public, a wave of parents sought the same therapy for their children, believing it to be a miracle cure. However, Charly warned that growth hormone only worked for those with a true deficiency. "For Messi, it was imperative," he explained. "Without it, he would not have reached his genetically intended height."

The future was uncertain, but this was the first step toward something extraordinary.

When the neighborhood kids said their goodbyes, his childhood friend remembered him trying to comfort them. "He hugged me and said, 'Don't cry, don't cry.'" But as the Messi family left Las Heras, his brothers and parents by his side, the pain was overwhelming. "Matías and I cried, we cried a lot," he recalled years later.

The journey to Barcelona felt like an exile, a dreamlike blur of sadness and uncertainty. Leaving behind friends, uncles, and the streets where he had grown up, he carried with him the weight of home—and the echoes of a life left behind.

Lionel Messi's departure from Rosario left deep scars, not only for his family but for those who had nurtured his talent. His coach once resented losing him, knowing that something special had happened at Newell's. The officials who failed to secure his future still carry receipts, trying to justify decisions that now seem like the greatest mistake in football history.

Messi, however, remained diplomatic. "Angry? No, because I'm not like that," he said in 2009. "I have a lot of love for the club. I went to the pitch as a small boy and dreamed of being on it one day."

The Road to Barcelona

So on September 16, 2000, Lionel Messi and his father, Jorge, boarded a transatlantic flight from Rosario to Barcelona.

Waiting at El Prat airport was their local contact, ready to take them to the Plaza Hotel. From his window, Messi looked out at the city that could become his new home. If things went well, there would be a contract, a house, a job for his father, and perhaps even a place in the club for his older brother, Rodrigo.

It was a bold move for a family to stake everything on a thirteen-year-old. Years earlier, Jorge and Celia had considered emigrating to Australia in search of better opportunities, but now, Barcelona seemed like the right choice. If Leo could continue his footballing development at a great club while receiving medical treatment, the sacrifice would be worth it. Still, the family questioned whether they were making the right decision. Before leaving, they gathered to discuss it, vowing that if even one of them objected, they would stay in Rosario.

For months, the Messi family had been cautious about empty promises from agents and scouts claiming to secure a European trial for Leo.

At just thirteen, Messi was already a sensation in youth football, with newspapers dedicating pages to his performances. River Plate had shown interest, but no solid offers had materialized.

Lionel Messi had been in Barcelona for two weeks, far longer than necessary for anyone to see his talent. But there were complications: he was foreign, too young, too small, and FIFA regulations required Barcelona to find his father a job. The club was already struggling, and many questioned whether signing a 13-year-old was worth the trouble.

But in August, an opportunity arose. Through connections in Barcelona, Messi was invited to trial with FC Barcelona. Signing foreign kids was not standard policy, let alone a non-EU player. "He'd have to be absolutely phenomenal for us to take an interest," Charly admitted.

The trial was set for September 18. Messi marveled at the facilities, posing for photos outside the Miniestadi, where Barça's youth teams played. Over the next week, he trained and played with kids his age. Under his father's watchful eye, he scored five goals in a single match, earning a promised tracksuit as a reward. The coaches were impressed, but the final decision rested with Charly, Barcelona's technical director.

Charly was in Australia for the Olympic Games, so Messi's stay in Barcelona was extended. On October 3, a special match was arranged against older players. Charly arrived late, running along the sidelines to reach the bench. But before he even sat down, his mind was made up. "We have to sign him. Now," he told the other coaches.

Messi's talent was undeniable. Small but fearless, he played with remarkable confidence, weaving past defenders with ease. "Some players need a team to shine—not him," Charly later recalled. "If a Martian had seen him play, they would have known he was special."

With the decision made, Messi and his father flew back to Argentina, assured that they would soon return to formalize the contract. The adventure had begun well, but there were still major hurdles: Messi was a foreign minor, ineligible for national competition, and his family needed jobs. And then, there was the issue of his costly medical treatment.

Despite the risks, Charly knew they had to sign him—because he was just that good.

The Napkin That Changed Football

Not everyone at Barcelona was convinced about signing Lionel Messi. Some saw him as too small, just another "nifty little player" who might not make it. When club president Joan Gaspart questioned the wisdom of committing to a thirteen-year-old and his family, Charly stood firm. "Bring me all the little players," he insisted. "I want them all in my team."

Messi returned to Rosario with a promise: "Don't worry, we'll sort everything out, and you can come back soon." But weeks passed. Then months. There were whispers that Barcelona had lost interest. The Messis waited, growing restless. An ultimatum was sent: either Barcelona committed, or they would look elsewhere. AC Milan, Atlético Madrid, and even Real Madrid were watching.

Charly knew time was running out. On December 14, ten weeks after Messi's trial, he met with agents Minguella and Gaggioli at a tennis club. After a game of doubles, they had beers. The conversation turned to Messi. "We ought to call the family," Minguella urged. "We keep telling them yes, but we haven't signed anything."

Gaggioli pressed harder. "Charly, either we commit today, or that's it—we go our way, they go theirs."

Charly, impatient and decisive, called for a pen and paper. But the club's offices were closed, and all they had was a napkin.

"In Barcelona on 14 December 2000, in the presence of Messrs Minguella and Horacio Gaggioli, the technical director of FCB commits to the signing of Lionel Messi, as long as the figures previously agreed are respected."

He signed it, along with Minguella and Gaggioli. Then it was notarized and locked away. It was a gentleman's agreement, the kind sealed with a handshake. For some, it became the most important document in Barcelona's modern history. For others, it was just a piece of paper.

The Messis never saw the napkin. But it was real. And it changed everything.

The napkin wasn't enough. The Messi family needed guarantees—a home, schooling, and a job for Jorge, who was leaving his work at Acindar. On January 8, 2001, the final agreement was reached in Via Veneto, a Barcelona restaurant. Jorge Messi was offered a position with the club, earning seven million pesetas (about £40,000), while the family's living arrangements were secured.

With the deal in place, the Messis finally made their move. On February 15, 2001, in the heart of winter, the entire family arrived in Barcelona, ready to start a new life.

CHAPTER 3
BARCELONA'S GAMBLE

A New Challenge in Barcelona

Adapting to life in Barcelona was the hardest part. The club had arranged a spacious apartment for the Messi family near Camp Nou, providing comfort and convenience. Lionel could wake up just 15 minutes before training and still make it on time. But while Rosario had treated him like a prodigy, in Barcelona, he was just another kid. Even the building concierge, years later, had no idea the polite boy he greeted each morning played for Barcelona.

From the start, things were tough. "I didn't understand a word—they all spoke in Catalan," Messi recalled. His teammates were indifferent, reluctant to pass him the ball. He was there to replace one of their friends, and that made him an outsider. He later learned that a coach had even instructed players to go in hard on him, hoping he wouldn't stay. But Messi ignored the hostility. "I just did what came naturally to me," he later said.

As a foreign player, Messi was ineligible for official matches with Infantiles A, the team of his age group. He played only in friendlies and the Catalan regional league. The coach Borrell was cautious, instructing defenders not to tackle him too hard. "He's so fast and small, you could hurt him," he warned. A towering teammate joked, "How can we be careful? We can't even get close to him!"

Despite initial doubts, Messi's talent became impossible to ignore. "He would pick up the ball and dribble past everyone," recalled another teammate. "We had never seen anything like it." Initially labeled as an individualist, his teammates soon realized his brilliance.

To challenge the squad, Borrell sent them to the tournament in Portugal to face older opponents. Messi, allowed to play since it wasn't an official competition, thrived. They finished third, and Leo proved he could compete at a higher level.

Still lacking international transfer papers from Newell's, Messi received a provisional license from the Catalan Federation on March 6. To ensure he played regularly, Barcelona moved him to Infantiles B—the only time in his career he played as the oldest in a group.

A coach's report confirmed what many had started to see: the quiet, 1.47-meter-tall boy was a "little Maradona," small in stature but with incredible skill. Messi made his official debut for Infantiles B, scoring in his first match.

A few weeks later, he played beside taller teammates. Though he had just arrived, his presence was undeniable. He was making Barcelona his home.

The game kicked off, marking Messi's second official match for Barcelona's Infantiles. It was more than just another game—it fulfilled a crucial requirement by the Spanish Federation, allowing him to progress through the club's ranks. If he hadn't played these two matches, he would have been forced to skip vital developmental stages, jumping straight from Cadetes to Barcelona B, a leap that could have jeopardized his growth as a player.

This rule had already derailed the career of another young foreign player. Without realizing the requirement, Barcelona failed to get him into Infantiles, forcing him to take a different path. Unlike Messi, he never made it back to the club's system and eventually faded into lower leagues. Sometimes, success and failure hinge on the smallest details.

Then came Messi's setback.

Seconds into the match, Messi lost control of the ball on the left wing. As Marc Baiges, his opponent, attempted to clear it, Messi instinctively stuck out his foot. The impact fractured his left fibula—the first serious injury of his career. Years later, Baiges was shocked when he learned what had happened: "I didn't even know I'd broken anyone's leg, let alone Messi's!" It wasn't even a foul.

On the bench, his coach saw it happen and knew immediately that something was wrong. Messi winced in pain but stayed composed, only asking how long he'd be out. The answer was two months. His father stayed by his side at the hospital, while the rest of the team finished the match.

Messi had to wear a plaster cast. He hobbled into training on crutches, unable to play. His teammates noticed his frustration, but his sister saw the deeper pain. On long afternoons, she would quietly hold his hand, sensing how much he longed to be on the pitch.

Just as he recovered, another blow struck. In June, a week after returning, he strained ligaments in his left ankle—going down the stairs. Three more weeks out. His body wasn't just small; it was fragile.

Four months in Barcelona, and Messi had played just two official matches and one friendly tournament. That summer, the Messi family returned to Rosario, their future uncertain. Messi's mother had left earlier to care for her sister, who needed surgery, and back home, there was comfort in familiar surroundings.

But something had shifted. The excitement of Barcelona had dimmed. At just 14, Messi stood at a crossroads. Would he return, or was his dream slipping away?

Struggles and Uncertainty

Before the family left Rosario, Jorge had reached out to a distant cousin, hoping for some support. But when they arrived in Spain, they had no safety net—just the five of them in a small apartment on Gran Via Carles III. They leaned on each other, trying to stay positive despite mounting challenges.

Leo longed to see the sea, something he had never known in Rosario. "We'd go to the beach," he later recalled. "It was cold, which made it a bit sad, but I liked it." These simple family outings were a rare comfort in an otherwise difficult period.

The reality of their new life was hitting hard. Messi couldn't play football, the very reason they had moved. Barcelona was slow to process his paperwork, and the club had not yet honored its financial promises. Jorge, struggling to keep the family afloat, wrote a desperate letter to club president Joan Gaspart on July 9, 2001, later published in El Gráfico:

"My situation and that of my family is desperate. I have made all necessary economic provisions up to this month, at which point the signed agreements should have taken effect. Now, I find myself without notice of any new payments and without anyone to guide me on what I should do."

The family felt abandoned—not necessarily by Barcelona as a club, but by those who had assured them everything would be taken care of. Leo was the club's main concern, monitored at school, in training, and for his health. But his siblings were struggling: Rodrigo couldn't continue playing football, María Sol faced discrimination at school, and Matías felt isolated after leaving his girlfriend in Rosario. The family's unity was unraveling.

Meanwhile, Barcelona itself was in turmoil. The first team struggled for trophies, and within the club, Messi was seen as a gamble—perhaps a future star, but just as likely another unfulfilled talent. To many, he was merely an investment. The board lacked the foresight to handle him properly, and the Messis were left to wonder if they had made the right choice in coming to Spain.

The Weight of Expectation

In 2009, during a TV interview, Messi was asked to say a simple phrase in Catalan: "Good night, I am Lionel Messi." He hesitated after "Bona nit", unable to finish. The audience laughed, but it was a reminder of how distant he still felt from the culture around him.

And yet, in 2012, when the Spanish government sought to restrict Catalan in schools, Messi publicly defended the language. In an event for Turkish Airlines, when asked about the proposed Education Act, he responded:

"Since I arrived in Catalunya, I have grown, studied, and learned in Catalan. The more languages a boy knows, the better for him."

It was an answer that pleased everyone. But eleven years earlier, the sense of alienation had been so strong that half of the Messi family wanted to return to Argentina for good.

At Lleó XIII school, Messi found little joy. He attended because it was expected of him, but his heart was elsewhere. Books sat open but unread, his mind consumed with training and football. He was not lazy—just disinterested. He complied, knowing that it was part of the path to professional football, but school never captured his attention the way the ball did.

Sometimes he missed the school bus, preferring to either train or rest. The PlayStation filled his free hours. He had finished his first year of secondary school in Rosario, but in Barcelona, he abandoned his studies just two years short of completing them. Though he excelled in gymnastics, his childhood dream of becoming a PE teacher faded. His mother wished he took his education more seriously—just in case football didn't work out—but as his future in the sport became more certain, school lost its relevance.

Yet school was not just dull; it was difficult. In Rosario, football had made him admired and accepted. But in Barcelona, surrounded by talented teammates, he was just another kid with an accent, different customs, and a growth condition. He was mocked, made to feel like an outsider. He withdrew, becoming quieter, more reserved. He listened more than he spoke, observed rather than participated. Away from football, he seemed detached, lost. His father saw him as responsible beyond his years, his mother described him as strong but quiet. But Leo was, above all, a boy in exile.

In Argentina, football had been joy, a dream he shared with his father and brothers. He had imagined making it to Newell's first team, like any other kid from Rosario. But now, at just 12 years old, football had become a serious choice. The opportunity to move abroad had forced a decision: yes or no. Did he want to be a professional? The only answer was yes.

Failure was not an option. His father had left his job, his mother had sacrificed her family, his brothers had left their friends. If he failed, what would become of them? For many young players, the burden of expectation stifles them. But for Messi, it planted a seed—a refusal to consider failure. Even at 11, he had proclaimed that he wanted to win the Ballon d'Or. Now that was no longer a childhood fantasy; it was a necessity.

For those who sacrifice everything, failure is unthinkable. They wake up each day believing in success, knowing that if they falter, their world could collapse. This belief, this unshakable mindset, does not just eliminate doubt—it suppresses emotion. To succeed, Messi had to become immune to fear, to pressure, to failure itself.

The Crossroads

At the end of a difficult season, the Messi family returned to Rosario for the summer, hoping to find clarity. The biggest decision had to be made: Messi's siter María would stay in Argentina. She had struggled to adapt to life in Barcelona, and no one wanted to see her unhappy any longer. But what about Messi?

Jorge Messi recalls the moment in Informe Robinson:

"One day I asked Leo, 'Well, what do you want to do? The decision is yours. If you want to come back to Argentina, then we'll come back.'"

Jorge made it clear that whatever happened, his son had his full support. There were no guarantees of success—none at all. But at just 14, Messi had to make a choice: go back home with his family, or stay in Barcelona and continue chasing his football dream, even if it meant splitting the family.

Messi looked at his father and said, "No, I want to stay. I want to play football in Barcelona and I want to play in the first division."

And so the Messi/Cuccittinis would be separated.

They wanted to believe it would only be temporary. Unlike the Italian immigrants of the past, who left their families behind forever, the Messis were determined to reunite. But for now, Celia, Rodrigo, Matías, and María Sol returned to Rosario, while Jorge stayed in Barcelona with Leo.

The decision was hardest on Celia, who, like any Argentinian mother, was at the center of family life. Now, she would only see her son twice a year and speak with him over the phone. Rodrigo would eventually return to Barcelona, but for months, Leo and his father were alone in their four-bedroom apartment on Gran Via Carles III.

Leo has always been close to his mother, but it Jorge had been the authoritative figure. More than just a father, he became his manager, the one who made the big decisions. The sacrifices Jorge made were not lost on his son.

In Rosario, his brothers struggled with guilt. Matías later admitted:

"While Leo always says that the family is the most important thing to him, that we always helped him, I think that I left him on his own. That's why I don't like to remember that time too much."

Rodrigo also found the adjustment difficult. "We suffered in different ways. Unfortunately, we ended up parting, but we're always coming and going. We traveled twice a year."

Years later, Jorge Messi admitted that if he had to make the decision again, he would never have allowed the family to split.

Around this time, Lionel Messi was on the verge of joining Real Madrid.

CHAPTER 4
THE MAKING OF A PRODIGY

A Strained Negotiation

In the summer of 2001, as Leo Messi prepared to return to Barcelona, a new obstacle emerged. The club had a new general manager, Farguell, who reviewed Messi's initial contract and was startled by the financial commitment. The agreement, drawn up months earlier, guaranteed Messi 100 million pesetas per season—an excessive amount for a young player who had yet to fully integrate into the system. Farguell decided to renegotiate.

Barcelona had been burned before. The club had previously paid high wages to young talents like, only for them to struggle and never reach the expected heights. The club was wary of repeating past mistakes. Messi's father, Jorge, was told that there was now a salary cap for academy players, limiting wages to 20 million pesetas (€120,000) per season—far less than what had been initially promised.

What followed was a series of difficult meetings. The club assembled a group of directors and agents to discuss the matter, but an agreement remained elusive. Tensions escalated when a club official, frustrated by Jorge Messi's firm stance, dismissed the situation outright: "Who does he think he is, Maradona? Let's close this now, and he can go back to Argentina."

That comment reflected the club's attitude at the time—there was no urgency, no sense of appreciation for the sacrifices the Messis had made. Jorge felt betrayed, realizing that those he had trusted had misled him. Meanwhile, negotiations remained at a standstill.

It was during this uncertain period that Real Madrid made their move. Madrid's sporting director let it be known that the club was willing to offer Messi the 20 million pesetas per season that Barcelona was now hesitant to pay. There was no formal offer, but the message was clear—if Messi became a free agent, Madrid would welcome him.

For the first time, there was serious talk of leaving Barcelona. "I think we'll go to Madrid," someone murmured in one of the meetings.

The threat of losing Messi finally forced Barcelona into action. After months of stalling, Farguell sat down with Jorge Messi and learned the truth: Jorge wasn't demanding millions for his son. All he wanted was a job, a stable home, and the continued payment of Leo's medical treatment.

Messi's representatives had previously promised Jorge a lucrative deal, claiming Messi would earn 100 million pesetas and that Jorge would secure a well-paying job at the club. Neither promise had materialized. When Jorge discovered the reality—hidden commissions, financial mismanagement, and false assurances—it shattered his trust. That was the moment he decided to personally handle all of Messi's affairs from then on, cutting ties with the intermediaries.

Legal battles followed, as some of these former representatives pursued claims against the Messis, but multiple court rulings sided with the family.

With the truth laid bare, Pérez Farguell agreed to a revised contract. Jorge Messi was given a job with a monthly salary of €3,900, while Messi's earnings were tied to his progress—his wages would increase depending on his performance and the level at which he played. To further support the family, the club even provided a loan for renovations on their Barcelona apartment.

On December 5, 2001—nine months after Messi's first contract—he finally had a stable agreement. The crisis was over.

And there was no need to return Madrid's call.

A Boy Far from Home

Years later, Messi reflected on his early days in Barcelona, alone with his father. "When I left, I cried a lot, I cried for everything I was leaving in Argentina, but at the same time, I had a dream and knew it was for the better." Sometimes, he would hide in his room, not wanting his father to see his tears.

"I locked myself in and cried."

At Barcelona, the routine was the same for all young players: school in the morning, training in the afternoon, and resting at La Masía. Most of his teammates lived in the academy, but Messi often went home to eat with his father. Alone, he passed the time watching TV, playing PlayStation, or taking naps before walking to training. Over time, he grew more comfortable, sometimes having breakfast at La Masía, where a teacher helped those players—like him—who lacked the motivation to keep up with school. But still, many hours remained empty.

With half his family back in Argentina, the time without football felt heavier. Jorge did what he could to keep Leo entertained—challenging him on the PlayStation, walking through the city, or taking him to shops. But there were no fields, no impromptu games with friends. Jorge became his son's only company, his playmate, his moral support.

At an age when most boys push against their parents, Messi leaned on his father more than ever. He had responsibilities beyond his years— he wasn't just a kid chasing a dream; he was the reason his family had split. This dynamic blurred the lines between father and manager. Jorge wanted Messi to stay humble, to respect his roots, and he instilled in him a deep sense of responsibility. But the balance was delicate. Overprotection was inevitable.

The siblings, too, lived in this strange balance. "We wouldn't live like this without you," they thought. "But our lives have always revolved around you." Being the brother of Lionel Messi was both a blessing and a burden.

But in the end, there was one small stroke of luck. Argentina's financial crisis had made life back home difficult, but because Jorge was earning in Spain, the money he sent back was worth double. Celia and the kids could live comfortably in Rosario on just half his salary.

Matías taught their mother how to use a webcam so she could see Leo online. They spoke every day, and he called every three days. But no matter how often they talked, Celia cried every time she heard his voice. And every time she saw him on TV.

Neither the players nor the coaches at La Masía knew that Leo cried at night alone in his bedroom. He kept his emotions locked away, presenting a calm and composed exterior. "It seemed like he was managing everything quite well," recalled one of his academy coaches. "I think he was very clear about one thing: he knew what he'd done: 'I have been separated from my mother and my brothers because I want to be a footballer; I don't know how far I'll get, or how long I'll last, but I know that I want it.'"

He understood that sacrifices had to be made, but he never let his doubts show. When asked how he was coping so far from home, he simply replied, "Well, my mother is coming now with my brothers."

Despite this, small clues revealed his inner turmoil. After long training sessions—three hours including warm-ups, exercises, and showers—Leo would always stay behind on the pitch, reluctant to leave. Football was his refuge, the only place where he could momentarily forget the weight of his sacrifice.

At just 14, he even handled interviews with remarkable maturity. When the television station TV3 visited him in his flat, he spoke confidently about his arrival in Spain and his early days at Barcelona. He answered carefully, with no hint of the stress his family was enduring. He knew he had to keep his head down, train harder than anyone else, and never let his struggles show.

He spent long evenings alone in his apartment with only his father's "goodnight" breaking the silence. Sundays were the hardest, stretching endlessly after morning games. To escape the solitude, he would take his time over lunch at Argentinian restaurants, play Xbox with teammates, or immerse himself in Argentinian television and films. His favorite movies, El hijo de la novia and Nueve reinas, featured Ricardo Darín, an actor he admired.

Despite living in Spain, Leo never lost his Rosario accent or customs. He sought out familiar comforts, frequenting Argentinian restaurants in Barcelona, where he would be the last to leave, savoring the feeling of home. Preserving his identity became essential to him. Many South American players come to Europe for success but dream of returning home. Leo, though different from the typical Argentinian, shared this deep-rooted attachment.

While Barcelona's official language was Catalan, the club never pressured him to speak it. The local Argentinian community also provided support, helping him feel less adrift in a foreign land. At the club's request, he began having breakfast at La Masía as part of a structured diet plan designed to support his growth. Meanwhile, club doctor Josep Borrell gradually reduced his growth hormone treatment, believing a controlled diet and proper fitness program would help him reach his full height naturally.

"In Spain, he grew in a way that you wouldn't believe," Jorge Messi later recalled. Over 29 months, Leo grew 29 centimeters. Yet, he frequently indulged in oversized Scaloppine Milanese and dulce de leche at his favorite Argentinian spots, embracing the tastes of home even as his body transformed.

A turning point came when his older brother, Rodrigo, returned to Barcelona permanently with his wife and their baby son. This reunion brought warmth to Messi's life. He spent countless hours with his nephew, taking on the role of a devoted caretaker. "While my sister-in-law makes dinner, I am with the boy. It's always me who puts him to bed at night. At first, I used to sing him lullabies, but my brother, my sister-in-law, and even the baby would laugh, so now I just walk around the house with Agustín in my arms, and he soon falls asleep," he shared in 2005.

Messi endured both physical and emotional hardships before reaching the top. His story is one of perseverance, resilience, and an extraordinary ability to push through pain. But for many years, despite his rising stardom, he never stopped crying after phone calls with his mother.

CHAPTER 5
MESSI'S BREAKTHROUGH

A Year of Challenges and Triumphs

At Can Vidalet Stadium, Messi debuted in the national championship against Esplugues de Llobregat.

Recovered from his injuries, Leo Messi began the 2001–02 season with the Junior B side. He trained alongside a historic generation of footballers, who played in the academy's signature 3-4-3 formation, producing one of the greatest youth teams Barcelona had ever seen. Yet, Messi's journey was still fraught with obstacles.

Due to ongoing transfer issues, he remained ineligible for national competitions and could only play sporadically. When he did, he was positioned on the left wing rather than his preferred role as an enganche, playing between the lines. "He loved cutting inside and creating chances," his coach recalled. But he had to adapt to the team's tactical needs. Off the pitch, Messi remained quiet and often appeared distant, even among his teammates.

Despite these challenges, the team dominated their competition. Traditionally, Junior A teams from Barcelona and Espanyol battled for the league title. However, Messi's Junior B side, playing against older opponents, made history by winning the championship. In the decisive match, they secured a 3–0 victory over Espanyol. They also claimed the Catalonia Cup, marking an extraordinary season, though they fell short in the Nike Cup semi-finals.

Midway through the season, a crucial development occurred: FIFA ruled in favor of Barcelona in its dispute with Newell's, allowing Messi's long-delayed transfer to be registered. On February 15, 2002, he officially joined the Spanish Football Federation. A year after arriving in Barcelona, he was finally free to play without restrictions.

At the next training session, their new coach gathered the team. "Boys," he said with a serious tone, "we have a new player with us." The team looked around, puzzled. "Leo Messi. Leo is our signing." The entire squad erupted in applause, celebrating their long-awaited teammate's full integration into the team.

Coming off the bench in the second half, he scored three goals in a 14–1 victory.

Messi's coach started playing him as a number 9, positioning him centrally for the first time. This false nine role allowed him to move between the lines, making him harder to mark. The defensive midfielder shifted to a more advanced playmaker role behind Messi.

The Reserved Prodigy

In the beginning, Leo Messi remained on the periphery of the dressing room, changing in a corner, avoiding interactions with his teammates. There seemed to be an invisible barrier around him, a quiet detachment that made him stand apart. While others chatted about their lives, Messi entertained himself with the ball at his feet, always close, as if it were his only companion. He rarely lingered in the dressing room after training, often rushing to meet his father outside. His teammates initially mistook his reserved nature for aloofness.

It was player Gerard Piqué who finally broke the ice, playing a harmless prank by hiding Messi's clothes. When the nervous young Argentine searched for them, the laughter quickly turned into reassurance. "Where are you from? What brings you here?" Piqué asked, welcoming him into the group. Messi's response was quiet. "Sorry, I'm just quiet." But from that point on, he spoke a little more. "We thought he was mute," joked a teammate, Cesc, later.

They gradually learned that his quiet demeanor wasn't arrogance but a deeply ingrained trait. He wasn't one to command the dressing room, rallying his teammates with motivational speeches. Instead, he spoke through his performances on the pitch. At first, his smaller physique was a challenge, but as he developed, his explosiveness set him apart. It wasn't until a few tournaments with the Junior B team that he fully opened up to his teammates.

His family insisted that Messi is not shy—just reserved. It was a behavior shaped in Argentina, where he was taught to respect the group, do his job, and let his football speak for itself. His immigrant status only reinforced this instinct. Like many young migrants, he matured faster, learning survival skills in an unfamiliar world. Merging into the background, avoiding conflict, and relying on his family became his defense mechanisms.

Cesc, who knew Messi well, once explained, "Leo is smart. He knows when to joke, when to be serious. Many of us speak without thinking, but he always knows what to say and when to say it." Even as a teenager, Messi understood the importance of timing—on and off the pitch.

Yet, in the end, he was still just a boy, far from home, carrying dreams bigger than himself. Even as Messi grew into a formidable player, part of him remained the same boy who hated losing, who got frustrated when substituted, and who carried his emotions onto the pitch. His family and club understood that this was not a flaw but a crucial part of his character—his raw love for the game. If that fire ever faded, Messi wouldn't be Messi anymore.

Because that child within him still existed, he cried—not just in private moments of homesickness but also in the face of defeat. Player Víctor recalls a league match against Espanyol when they were 15 years old. Barcelona lost, and though the result wasn't decisive, Messi sat in the dressing room, silent, his head bowed, his shirt pulled over his face. When Víctor nudged him, Messi's tear-filled eyes met his. "I'm sorry," he muttered, "I couldn't score. I feel really bad." His frustration wasn't about himself but about letting the team down.

Víctor tried to console him. "We'll win the next one," he reassured. And they did. In the following match, Messi scored a hat-trick. As the season wound down, Barcelona overtook Espanyol and won the league. Messi was the first to say, "See how everything can change?"

As he matured, Messi learned that he wasn't the center of the universe—that losses, setbacks, and failures were part of the journey. When he traveled to Italy with the Junior A team for a tournament, he finally started integrating, no longer the quiet outsider. The trip to Pisa proved a turning point; spending every moment with his teammates, sharing jokes, and living as one of them, he finally began to feel like he belonged.

Messi's Turning Point in Pisa

The Junior side was invited to compete in the Maestrelli trophy in Pisa. Messi, wearing the number 14 shirt, dominated the tournament, finishing as both top scorer and best player. Barcelona won the final against Parma 2–0, and Leo also secured victory in the PlayStation league among his teammates.

During the trip, his teammates took things to another level. They completely emptied Messi's hotel room—his PlayStation, clothes, bed, everything. When Leo returned after lunch, expecting his usual siesta, he found the room bare. His eyes widened in shock, and, believing he had been robbed, he threw himself to the floor in distress. The coach recorded the whole thing, laughing as Messi panicked. They eventually told him the truth, but only after letting him suffer for a few hours.

Though it was a prank, this moment marked a shift in Messi's integration into the team. He understood that being the target of a joke meant acceptance. From then on, he began participating in the group's humor, pulling small pranks of his own. While never as outspoken as the others, he laughed more and engaged with his teammates beyond just football. The PlayStation remained his greatest pastime, and during the trip, he proved unbeatable, frustrating his friends as he played for hours without losing.

Two of Messi's closest friends in Barcelona, were the first to call him "enano"—dwarf—a nickname he took in stride. He retaliated by confusing them with Argentine slang they couldn't understand. This playful exchange was a sign of trust, a key moment in his slow but steady acceptance within the group.

Cesc later recalled, "Leo opened up… imagine just how much he opened up that everyone remembers that trip." The shy, reserved boy was still quiet, but something had changed in Italy. At Barcelona airport, when a teammate hesitated to ask a stranger for something, Messi unexpectedly stepped in, showing a new confidence.

Back in Barcelona, his once-quiet flat became the meeting place for the next PlayStation showdown.

Messi's Growing Place in the Team

As time passed, the team developed a natural rhythm, each player settling into his role. The generation of '87 spent over two years together before his friends left, and in that time, Messi transformed from an outsider into a key player. Yet, perceptions of him remained mixed.

In Rosario, he was protected—coaches, referees, and friends all shielded him. In Spain, however, his quiet nature, immense talent, and evolving physique created contradictions. Some teammates believed he needed no special treatment, competing against him as equals. Others still felt the urge to protect him.

Though Messi was growing, some continued to recognize his fragility. He was no longer just the shy boy in the background—he was proving his worth on the field. The team was beginning to gel, and Messi was finding his place, even as he remained somewhat enigmatic to those around him.

During the 2002–03 season, Messi and his teammates moved up to Junior A under Alex García. One unforgettable match was a youth clásico against Damm, where Barcelona led 6–0. Despite the comfortable lead, Messi kept attacking, cutting in from the left, determined to take on defenders one-on-one. But the opposition responded with brutal tackles—again and again.

"They kicked him mercilessly," recalled Víctor. "But he just kept getting up." 'The Flea' was furious—not because of the kicks, but because he wanted to keep playing. "Most players would want to come off," Víctor said. "But not him. He would've played on another wing if needed—he just wanted to play."

CHAPTER 6
BREAKOUT SEASON

Masked Final

Those who witnessed the match still recall it with awe. It was the final game of the season between Barcelona and Espanyol, two fierce rivals. Although Barcelona had already secured the league title, pride was at stake. The Junior A side led 1–0 when Messi chased a long ball, leaped to control it, and collided with an Espanyol defender. The sound of impact echoed across the field.

Messi crashed to the ground, motionless. Blood streamed from his nose. His father, Jorge, sprinted onto the pitch, panic-stricken. The doctor confirmed the worst—a fractured cheekbone. Messi was rushed to the hospital, where he was told he'd be out for eight weeks. Yet, even in his hospital bed, his only concern was missing the Catalonia Cup final the following week. When he visited his teammates, he downplayed the pain. "I don't like being injured," he admitted.

His determination caught the attention of the club captain, who had suffered a similar injury earlier in the season. The club's medical staff retrieved the captain's protective mask and told Messi he could play— on one condition: he had to wear it. His coach, warned him, "If you don't follow the rules, you're off." Messi nodded, but his frustration was clear.

The final arrived, and Messi started, adjusting the mask constantly. Seven minutes in, he lost the ball while trying to fix it. "I can't see anything," he told his coach. Moments later, ignoring medical advice, he ripped the mask off and tossed it to the bench.

What happened next was pure Messi. He dribbled past one defender, then another. He received a pass and scored. Minutes later, he danced past Espanyol's defense again and slotted another goal past the keeper. Two goals in ten minutes. Barcelona led 3–0 by halftime. The coach, worried for his health, subbed him out despite his protests. The game ended 4–1, sealing another title for Messi's team.

Reflecting on that day, the coach said, "At the partido de la máscara, I saw Messi wasn't just playing for himself—he was playing for the team. He was willing to do anything to win."

The first team of the club was in turmoil during the 2002-03 season. The manager's second tenure ended disastrously, with the team languishing in 13th place by January, leading to his dismissal. His successor could only manage a 6th-place finish, marking the club's worst performance in 15 years. Amidst this, the club president resigned, ushering in new leadership. This change was accompanied by a general sense of hope and anticipation for the arrival of a new star player, which was seen as a beacon for turning the club's fortunes around. The sentiment within and around the club was one of disappointment with the immediate past but optimism for the future under new management and with the promise of exciting new talent.

While the Camp Nou was filled with whistles and frustration, on the youth pitches, something special was happening.

The Junior A squad, featuring a golden generation of players including Messi, Cesc and Víctor, was maturing into a dominant force. The team was fiercely competitive, training with an intensity that sometimes exceeded their actual matches. "They were 15 or 16, but they had the mentality of professionals," the coach recalled. They never settled for a simple win—whether in training or competition, every goal mattered.

But among the three, Messi was exceptional. Leo played every match that season, scoring 36 goals—five more than centre-forward Víctor. "He was a small, quiet boy, but he listened, and I knew he listened because he applied what we discussed." A defining moment came in a match against a strong Damm side. Messi scored the opener with a nutmeg and added another in a dominant 3–0 win. "That's when I saw his true potential," the coach García said.

Messi preferred playing centrally rather than staying wide, instinctively drifting inside. García experimented with his positioning to develop his versatility. "You can't put the brakes on talent," he says. Alongside Víctor Vázquez, Messi formed an unstoppable partnership.

By now, Messi fully understood his importance to the team and his growing potential. Before a crucial league match, García reassured him to stay calm, but Leo confidently responded, "Don't worry, I'll sort this out." Within ten minutes, he had scored three goals, and Barcelona won 7–1.

That season, Messi and his Junior A side won everything: the league, the Championship of Spain, and the Championship of Catalonia— including the legendary "Final of the Mask."

From Youth Tournaments to Barcelona B

In August 2003, a Spanish newspaper ran the headline: 'Barça Dying for This Kid'. The article hailed Messi as a rising star, dazzling Barcelona's youth ranks after leaving Newell's at 13. At just 16, he was already drawing comparisons to Maradona. The piece described him as "pure potrero"—a left-footed, skilful, natural goalscorer shaped by Argentina's rugged street football. Barcelona's first team was in sight.

That season started with Leo joining the under-16 side under coach Guillermo Hoyos, an Argentinian and Newell's fan like Messi himself. Hoyos had never seen Leo play up close, but after just five minutes of training, he was in awe. What followed was something unprecedented in the Barcelona academy.

The Youth B side traveled to Japan for the Toyota International Youth U-17 Championship. In their first match, Barcelona struggled early, trailing by a goal. Frustrated, Leo took control, dribbling past four defenders and the goalkeeper before setting up Songo'o for an equalizer. He dominated the tournament, winning MVP honors. He repeated this feat in Sitges, Sant Vicenç de Montalt, and Italy's San Giorgio della Richinvelda tournament. In the latter, Barcelona scored 35 goals in five matches, conceding only a single corner. Messi missed a penalty in an earlier game, but when given another in the final against Juventus, he demanded the ball and scored.

Messi's manager saw something special in him. Though reserved, he led by example. For a few matches, he even wore the captain's armband. He turned to his assistant Ángel Alcolea and, with emotion in his voice, said: "I'm choked up, Ángel, this kid is just like Diego."

Preseason ended with just one loss, against Real Madrid. Around this time, Barcelona B coach spotted Messi by chance. His team was training on half a pitch while Messi's side used the other. The coach noticed a player who was "fast, electric, very active, dribbling past everyone and scoring." He was so impressed that he told his assistant, "I've seen a player from the under-16s who should train with us." The assistant was skeptical but agreed to watch Leo for a week. Soon after, he returned and said, "You know what? You're right. He should train with us."

The two approached the youth director with their request. Concerned about Messi's physique and adaptability, director hesitated but ultimately agreed. To mask Leo's rapid rise, they also promoted two other players. Thus, at just 16, Leo began training sporadically with

Barcelona B while playing for Junior A.

Gerard, who was also moved up to Junior A after Cesc left for Arsenal, recalled, "Leo and I were a gang." However, when Gerard's transfer to Manchester United was finalized in December, he was sent back to the under-16s. He still followed Messi's games closely, especially the Copa del Rey, where "it was Leo against the world." In a crucial match against Osasuna, Messi single-handedly won the game, proving once again that his talent was undeniable.

Messi netted 18 goals in 11 games for the under-17s, including a stunning left-footed strike from midfield in the final of a friendly tournament against Betis. Meanwhile, Barcelona C struggled, sitting bottom of their division after just one win in 15 games. Recognizing his potential, his coaches moved Messi up to the C team—his third squad of the season.

A coach recalled, "We were struggling, and Messi arrived like a breath of fresh air. He had an extra gear from everybody else." In his first match, Barça C won 3-1 against Europa. He scored five goals in ten games, including a quickfire brace against Gramenet that turned a losing match into victory.

In the Spanish Cup, he faced Sevilla and their right-back, a young Sergio Ramos. In just eight minutes, Messi scored a hat-trick. Ramos would never forget it.

Messi's Ascent

Messi continued making rapid progress, always positive and never complaining. "He loved football so much that he could never say no, no matter who the team was," said his coach. "He needed to get stronger, but he made us more competitive. When Messi had the ball, it was magical. The others watched him in awe, wanting to copy his movements." His presence created an atmosphere of fierce yet positive competition.

Despite advancing quickly, his physical frailty remained a concern. "We wanted to strengthen him," his trainers agreed. "Not with weights, but with exercises to ensure he could handle the physical demands of playing against fully grown men." He had stopped taking hormone injections at fourteen, and now his training had to match his body's natural growth.

Even before club specialists intervened, Messi and his father would go to an empty lot near Camp Nou, following a speed and stamina regimen. Later, under professional supervision, his focus shifted to power and agility, strengthening his lower body. He even sought extra guidance from a personal trainer, hoping to enhance his resilience while avoiding injury. And when he wasn't training, he was resting—a crucial part of his development. A daily siesta, often on the sofa at home, became a routine.

At Barcelona B training sessions, Messi often played on the right, mimicking the first team's system. "We replicated the senior squad," his coach recalled. "He would cut inside from the right, like his idol on the left, using his left foot to weave through defenders." Though excited, Messi initially felt out of place among older, more experienced players. Shy as ever, he kept his head down, changed quickly, and avoided drawing attention.

His Barcelona B debut was imminent. But before that—an unexpected surprise.

Path to Barcelona's First Team

Between August 2003 and April 2004, Messi gained 3.7 kilograms, mostly muscle. No longer the frail youngster, his growth came not from the gym but from intense training and regular starts for Barcelona B. His rapid rise was fueled by the unwavering belief of key coaches and the club's youth director, who assured Messi's father that he would only be stopped when his progression naturally reached its peak, not before. Confidence became his most vital asset.

During the 2004-05 season, Barcelona underwent significant restructuring, ensuring that the team revolved around player Ronaldinho. Key players departed, and fresh talent arrived, forming a core that brought renewed optimism to the club. With a dynamic midfield and an attacking trio led by Ronaldinho, Barcelona was poised for success.

Meanwhile, Messi, who had made his first-team debut in a friendly against Porto in 2003, found himself waiting for more opportunities. Despite his rapid progress, the doors to the first team remained largely closed. Doubts emerged both within the club and from his family—why wasn't he playing more? How was he handling the lack of chances?

For a teenager on the brink of elite football, it was a challenging period. To help him navigate the uncertainty, the club arranged for him to be assessed by an Argentinian psychologist, selected by the academy director. The intention was to ensure that he remained mentally strong amid the pressure and expectations surrounding his rise.

The transition to Barcelona B proved challenging for 17-year-old Messi. After his meteoric rise in the junior ranks, he struggled to make the same impact. Despite playing every minute, he scored only five goals in his first 12 matches. Defenders were stronger, space was harder to find, and he couldn't dominate as easily.

The team itself was also struggling. A 3-0 defeat in September left Messi devastated. Back in the dressing room, he broke down in tears, surprising his coach, who reassured him: "He played well! We had to tell him to persist and turn this loss into something positive." Unlike his teammates, for whom the game was just another match, Messi felt every setback deeply.

Gradually, his role at the club shifted. He trained daily with the B team but started joining first-team sessions once a week—then twice, then three times. The assistant coach remained cautious, insisting Leo still had areas to improve. But Ronaldinho pushed back, telling the staff: "Gaffer, he should be here, playing with us."

The assistant coach, known for his strict approach, believed the young Argentine was ready for the first team. He was often seen as the disciplinarian in contrast to the main coach's calm demeanor, responsible for keeping the squad focused. However, even he recognized that the young talent's promotion was imminent.

The Beginning of a Legend

In his early years, Messi resisted playing on the wing, preferring a central role where he could be more involved in the game. Coaches, however, often placed him wide on the right, knowing that his left-footed ability allowed him to cut inside and create chances. Despite this, he frequently drifted into the mediapunta zone, where he felt most at home. However, he understood that breaking into the first team required adaptation. With Ronaldinho dominating the left flank, Messi had no choice but to accept the role assigned to him. The priority was to reach the top and stay there.

Nearly a year after his debut in a friendly against Porto, Messi felt he was ready for his official breakthrough. So did the assistant coach. With Barcelona leading La Liga after six unbeaten games, Messi finally got his chance on 16 October 2004 in the derby against Espanyol. He entered the field in the final minutes with the instruction to exploit his speed between defenders.

Though his time on the pitch was brief, history was made. At just 17 years and four months, Messi became the youngest player to represent Barcelona in an official match.

That night, he returned home with his father. There were no celebrations—just quiet reflection. He had taken his first step, but in his mind, the journey was just beginning. The applause from the Camp Nou echoed in his memory.

In the following weeks, he played 20 minutes against Osasuna but remained on the bench for the next seven games. Sitting behind his coach, he watched Ronaldinho in his prime, dazzling the crowd. At the time, Messi didn't fully understand why he wasn't playing more. Years later, he would acknowledge his coach's patience: "He took me step by step, without pressure… I now realize he brought me along very well."

The coach, Rijkaard's management style was built on trust and care. Former teammates described him as more than just a coach— sometimes a mentor, a brother, or even a father figure. His patience helped shape Messi, ensuring that when his moment arrived, he was ready to embrace it.

Rijkaard instinctively extended his paternal approach to Messi. A hug, a joke before training, or a simple inquiry about his life off the pitch helped build a relationship of trust. Messi, naturally reserved, felt comfortable around him and remained forever grateful. Footballers never forget the coach who gives them their first real opportunity. "It doesn't matter if you make mistakes," Rijkaard reassured him. "You will play again." That faith gave Messi confidence.

Rijkaard understood those who were different. Coming from an immigrant background himself, he related to Messi's quiet nature, just as he had with Ronaldinho. He knew football belonged to the players, not the coaches, and his role was to guide, not control. This belief, paired with his honesty, made him a master at earning players' respect.

While he spoke more with senior players like Ronaldinho, he made a deliberate effort to connect with Messi. During team meetings, other players led the discussions, while Messi barely spoke unless directly asked. His responses were brief, reflecting his desire to follow orders rather than take the spotlight. Rijkaard used this dynamic wisely, easing Messi's transition into the club's elite.

CHAPTER 7
A NIGHT TO REMEMBER

The Unstoppable Competitor

On the morning of the match against Albacete, Messi left his apartment as he had done before every home game. Though he had played sparingly in the league, cup, and Champions League that season, he knew the routine. Arriving at the Camp Nou at 11 a.m., he had the option to work out in the gym, get a massage, or, like many of his teammates, engage in a competitive round of football tennis.

The game had started with Ronaldinho and Silvinho, who took advantage of an open space in the dressing room. They improvised a court with sticky tape lines and a bandage stretched across as a net. It became a serious competition, with Silvinho often outplaying Ronaldinho and claiming himself as the best—until Messi joined in.

Messi saw it as more than a game; it was another way to prove himself. Though he waited his turn at first, he quickly became the player everyone wanted to beat. He was relentless, precise, and, as always, obsessed with winning. His ability to place shots where they were impossible to reach gave him the edge. Even seasoned players spent hours trying to defeat him, only to be outclassed every time.

What started as fun became a test of skill, mentality, and determination. The coaches observed closely—watching Messi's intensity, competitiveness, and ability to stay focused under pressure. Even in a game played for laughs, he showed the same drive that would later define his career.

After training, the squad would head to the Princesa Sofia hotel for food and rest. But Messi had already won his first battle of the day.

The match against Albacete in May was a crucial one. With only four games left in the season, Barcelona needed to maintain their lead at the top. Madrid, fueled by players like Ronaldo, had won six consecutive matches and were closing in. Despite Albacete's struggles at the bottom of the table, the game proved tougher than expected. But Barcelona lacked rhythm and their creativity was met with resistance. The first breakthrough didn't come until the hour mark when Eto'o fired a shot past Valbuena.

With seven minutes left, Leo Messi was asked to warm up. Eto'o, visibly displeased, made it clear he wasn't ready to come off, but the change was inevitable. Rijkaard's instructions to Messi were simple: "Play how you know. Stick yourself on the right." Eto'o left the pitch furious, storming into the dressing room.

On the field, Ronaldinho saw an opportunity. "I'm going to give you a pass for you to score," he told Messi. "Tomorrow, you'll be on the front pages."

A perfect pass came, and Messi finished with a delicate lob over the goalkeeper—only for it to be ruled offside.

But Ronaldinho wasn't finished. Moments later, he lifted the ball over the defense again. This time, Messi let it bounce once before chipping it into the net. His first official goal for Barcelona.

The celebration was unforgettable. Arms outstretched, Messi ran before turning back, seeking his teammates. Ronaldinho rushed over, bent forward, and Messi jumped onto his back. The fans roared, chanting his name. The league title was within reach.

In the dressing room, the atmosphere was electric. Players congratulated him, joking with Ronaldinho that his position might be in danger. In the press area, Messi dedicated his goal to his mother, who was traveling, and to his soon-to-be-born nephew.

His father, Jorge, still got goosebumps thinking about that night. "You hear the people singing 'Messi, Messi, Messi.' It's the biggest thing that can ever happen to anybody."

That night, Messi ate dinner, went to bed, and woke up to a phone call. On the other end was Diego Maradona, calling to congratulate him. It was the first time they had spoken. It wouldn't be the last.

A Champion's Summer

Barcelona had won their first league title in five years, and though Leo Messi had played just 77 minutes for the first team—including a Champions League debut—he celebrated like a veteran. On the open-top victory bus, he danced alongside the Brazilians, who had affectionately named him irmão (little brother). He was the team's mascot, grinning from ear to ear, soaking in the moment.

At the Camp Nou, news reached him that his sister-in-law, had gone into labor. Without hesitation, Messi left the celebrations. That night, his nephew, Agustín, was born. After all the excitement, he returned to Rosario for a well-earned break.

Rijkaard, reflecting on the season, believed Messi was still not fully ready. He wanted to shield him, allow him time to mature. But Messi had no doubts. At 17, he knew he belonged. His performances with Barcelona B, where he had played 17 matches and nearly helped them secure promotion, had proven that he was beyond the reserve level.

After resting, he set off for the Under-20 World Cup in Holland. He didn't just win the title—he was named the best player of the tournament.

A Life in Fast Forward

The summer of 2005 was a whirlwind for Leo Messi, a turning point in his career where everything seemed to accelerate overnight. No longer just a promising teenager, he was now an international star, a league champion, and a world champion with Argentina's Under-20 squad. But beyond the accolades, it was the changes in his status at Barcelona that truly defined this period.

His contract situation evolved rapidly. His first agreement with the club had been sealed on a napkin. By 2004, he had signed a deal structured around Barcelona's lower ranks, with clauses that adjusted based on whether he played for the C team, the B team, or the first team. His wages, buyout clauses, and even allowances for flights to Argentina reflected his uncertain position within the club hierarchy. At that stage, Messi was still negotiating from a position of weakness, grateful for any support Barcelona provided.

However, with his meteoric rise, the club's approach changed. Barcelona's management, recognizing both his talent and the sacrifices he had made, restructured his contract. His new deal, signed during the Under-20 World Cup, secured his place in the first team and increased his earnings significantly. More importantly, it signaled Barcelona's commitment to treating him as one of their stars. Yet even this contract was outdated before it took effect—within three months, it was rewritten to reflect his growing importance.

With his new status came new responsibilities. He was now part of Barcelona's elite squad, traveling on promotional tours as a full-fledged first-team player. The pre-season trip to Asia in the summer of 2005—through Korea, China, and Japan—was his first real taste of life as a global football icon. Fans clamored for him, brands wanted his image, and the demands of stardom began to shape his daily life.

But inside the team, Messi still leaned on his closest companions. He followed the Brazilian contingent everywhere, drawn to their relaxed attitude and playful nature. He was still reserved, still reluctant to speak too much in public, but among them, he found comfort. On the road, he relied on others to help him navigate new experiences. On one occasion, he struggled to communicate with a hotel cleaner in China, shouting "Go, go" in frustration while the worker, unable to understand him, continued his task. His teammates laughed as they watched the scene unfold, amused by Messi's bewilderment at the simplest of interactions in a foreign language.

For the first time, Messi had the security and prestige of being a recognized member of the first team. No longer a prospect waiting for a chance, he was now a player Barcelona was building their future around. His journey from an unknown teenager to a footballing phenomenon had happened in the blink of an eye.

The Night Messi Became a Star

On August 24, 2005, the Camp Nou hosted the Joan Gamper Trophy, Barcelona's annual pre-season showcase. The match was meant to introduce the squad to the fans, and while the spotlight was expected to be on the usual stars, it was a 17-year-old Lionel Messi who stole the show.

Rijkaard, in a show of faith, named Messi in the starting lineup. From the opening minutes, he was fearless. He demanded the ball, drifted across the pitch, initiated attacks from midfield, and dribbled past some of the best defenders in the world. At one point, he nutmegged the reigning world-class center-back. A frustrated player resorted to a cynical foul that earned him a yellow card—one of three Juventus players booked while trying to stop Messi. Despite their aggression, he remained unfazed, assisting the first goal and nearly scoring himself.

On the touchline, the Juventus manager was astonished. Standing beside Rijkaard, he made a bold request: "You can't keep this kid on the bench. Let me have him on loan for a year. In any other team, he'd be starting." Rijkaard declined. Barcelona's plan was clear—once the red tape preventing Messi from playing regularly was resolved, he would become a first-team fixture.

Juventus equalized, and the match ended 2–2, with the Italians winning on penalties. But the real takeaway was Messi's dazzling display. Named Man of the Match, he had captivated not just the fans, but football's elite. In the post-match press conference, the Juventus manager was effusive: "I've never seen a player with so much quality at that age, wearing such an important shirt. Messi is a great champion, a genius, someone who can decide any game."

That night, Messi's name crossed borders. Suddenly, he wasn't just a promising talent in Barcelona—he was a global sensation. Offers flooded in. Juventus put forward a serious bid, but it was Inter Milan that made the most audacious attempt, reportedly triggering his €150 million buyout clause. If the bureaucratic issues preventing Messi from playing in La Liga weren't resolved, he would leave for Italy.

At Barcelona, the Juventus manager's words had forced everyone to take notice. Until then, Messi had been a project, a player with enormous potential but still waiting for his moment. Now, there was no denying it—his time had come.

The Moment Messi Almost Left Barcelona

In September 2005, Lionel Messi was closer to leaving Barcelona than at any other time in his career. His meteoric rise had caught the attention of Europe's biggest clubs, and Inter Milan was prepared to break the bank to secure his signature. They saw a golden opportunity—a 17-year-old wonderkid unable to play in La Liga due to bureaucratic issues, his future uncertain. Their offer was staggering: three times his Barcelona salary and a willingness to trigger his €150 million buyout clause.

Jorge Messi, acting as both a father and an agent, took the matter seriously. He arranged a private meeting with Joan Laporta, Barcelona's president, presenting Inter's offer not as a demand, but as a decision that had to be made. Laporta, understanding the weight of the situation, spoke both as a club official and as someone who had built a personal relationship with Messi's family. He assured Jorge that Barcelona would take care of Leo financially, but more importantly, that Barcelona was the club where he would find both success and legacy. He argued that Inter could offer money, but Barcelona could give him glory.

For the moment, the discussion ended without resolution. But tensions escalated when Jorge Messi met with another sporting director in Germany, where Barcelona was preparing to play in the Champions League. Expecting a renewal proposal to reflect Messi's status as an international star and U-20 World Cup winner, he instead encountered reluctance. Barcelona had just given Messi a contract a few months prior, and they were in no rush to discuss a new one. Frustrated, Jorge Messi made it clear—if Barcelona didn't recognize Messi's worth, he would leave for Inter.

Behind the scenes, Inter was working fast. They had a concrete plan: if Messi's La Liga registration issues weren't resolved by December, he would move to Milan the following season. As negotiations stalled, Barcelona officials received a frantic call from Messi's camp—he was ready to go. Panic set in. Losing Messi, a player the club had nurtured since he was 13, would be an unthinkable disaster.

On the day of the Werder Bremen match, Rijkaard named Messi on the bench. In the 65th minute, he sent him on. The teenager immediately made an impact, taking on defenders, driving forward with purpose. Late in the game, after a clever pass from Ronaldinho, Messi broke free into the box, only to be pulled back by a desperate defender.

A clear penalty.

Ronaldinho stepped up and converted it, sealing a 2–0 win. In the stands, Barcelona executives saw the performance and knew—they couldn't afford to let him go.

The next morning, an emergency meeting was called at the Camp Nou. The key decision-makers sat down with Jorge Messi. The message was clear: Messi was Barcelona's future. Yes, Inter was offering astronomical sums, but La Liga suited his style. His development was happening within a system built for him. Here, he could become one of the greatest players in history.

Jorge Messi believed them. Messi's wanted to stay. The contract negotiations were fast-tracked, and Messi secured a place in the first-team squad. Just as crucially, the meeting established a direct line between Messi's family and the Barcelona president, so that future issues would be handled with care.

Barcelona had won the battle. The teenager who would go on to define an era remained at the club.

Inter Milan's attempt to lure Lionel Messi away from Barcelona fell short. While they were prepared to offer triple his salary, they hesitated at paying the full €150 million buyout clause. Instead, they considered challenging its validity in court, arguing that Messi's earnings were disproportionately low compared to what Barcelona was demanding for him. But when they learned that Messi and his father had ultimately decided to stay, they abandoned the pursuit.

With the transfer threat resolved, Barcelona swiftly worked on a new contract. Messi's rising stardom made his small apartment increasingly impractical, as evidenced by an incident where a fan jumped onto his car, refusing to leave until he got an autograph. To accommodate his growing profile, the new deal included a bonus to help finance a house in Castelldefels.

Messi and his father negotiated carefully. They initially sought a contract running until 2013, ensuring flexibility before the 2014 World Cup, which they saw as a crucial moment in his career. Barcelona, however, secured an extension until 2014. The revised deal significantly improved his financial standing. His salary started at €900,000 in the first year and would rise to €3.5 million by 2014, including image rights. Additional performance-based bonuses were included, alongside a one-time €2 million signing bonus.

Meanwhile, Barcelona worked to resolve Messi's bureaucratic issues. Having missed the first six La Liga games due to foreign player registration limits, the club had a backup plan. Years earlier, Jorge Messi had applied for Spanish nationality for his son, and after months of waiting, on 26 September 2005, Lionel Messi officially became a Spanish citizen.

Now, he was finally eligible to play.

CHAPTER 8
THE RISE OF A SUPERSTAR

Heartbreak and Hard Lessons

Leo Messi was determined to be fit for the Champions League final. The idea of playing in such a prestigious match thrilled him. His recovery routine was relentless—morning and afternoon training with his personal trainer, physiotherapy sessions, gym workouts, swimming, and strict rest. He could not afford to miss such a monumental moment, especially in a World Cup year.

By 10 April, a week before the semi-final against Milan and five weeks before the final, he was finally cleared to rejoin the squad. He had already missed crucial league games and the Champions League quarter-finals, but Rijkaard planned to ease him back, keeping him on the bench in Italy. Leo, however, was eager to return at full strength.

His coach skeptical of his readiness, consulted the medical staff. They confirmed he was cleared but recommended caution. When Messi insisted he was fine, his coach warned him not to push himself too hard. During the training session, Messi took a free-kick against advice. As soon as he struck the ball, he felt a sharp pain—the muscle had torn again.

Messi knew instantly what had happened. His dream of playing in the final collapsed in that moment. The club issued a vague statement, avoiding details, but the truth was clear: he had rushed back too soon. His muscles, still healing, had not yet regained the necessary oxygen levels for full exertion. At his age, the doctors noted, it was natural that he didn't fully understand his limits.

Returning home, Messi was devastated. He refused to speak to anyone. The injury meant restarting his entire rehabilitation process—morning physiotherapy, afternoon gym work, and strict rest. The same cycle all over again, with the final slipping out of reach.

Leo Messi and his trainer traveled to Rosario, far from those who might push him to return too soon. There, he watched his teammates make a beautiful goal against Milan, the one that secured Barcelona's place in the final. His reaction was quiet—a simple, muted "Goal." He was determined to be fit, to at least make the bench for the final. He worked relentlessly, believing he would make it.

Time was slipping away. The final was on 17 May, just five weeks after his last injury and three weeks after the semi-final. By early May, he felt strong again, eager to return. His trainer urged caution, but Messi insisted. He asked Rijkaard to include him in the squad. Three days before the final, he rejoined full training.

On 16 May, Rijkaard faced the media. He avoided discussing Messi's fitness, saying he would decide later. "Messi? We will see what happens tomorrow. He has only had two training sessions. You never know." That afternoon, Messi trained intensely in Saint-Denis, looking sharp and determined. He took a powerful shot that hit Eto'o, momentarily stunning him. His body felt strong. He was sure he was ready.

But his managers had already made their decision. After training, they called Messi into an empty dressing room. Rijkaard spoke first: he wasn't fully fit, and he wouldn't be included in the squad.

Messi's face tightened. His lips trembled, his eyes welled up. But he didn't argue. He inhaled deeply, then exhaled in silence. His tears began to fall.

The assistant coach later reflected, "Can you imagine? An 18-year-old kid missing a final because of his own miscalculations?" The staff saw it as a hard but necessary lesson. If Messi had listened to his body earlier, he could have been part of Barcelona's team chasing their second European Cup.

Other players accepted their fate more easily. Knowing they weren't at their best, they stayed on the bench, ready if needed. But Messi, an explosive player, couldn't do the same. The disappointment was unbearable.

For Messi, the coaching staff believed his exclusion was a lesson—he would learn to listen, not only to others but to his own body. But Messi couldn't enjoy the final. The game felt distant, even as he watched the players secure Barça's comeback victory.

When the final whistle blew, Messi didn't celebrate. He walked straight to the dressing room, his head down. The assistant manager, smoking in the tunnel, saw him pass by, his disappointment visible in every step.

He refused to hold the trophy, to wear his medal, to be in any photos.

Alone in the dressing room, he wept.

His trainer found him in a corner. "Leo, if you hadn't been fit for the Chelsea game, with that tackle and the red card… we wouldn't have made it here."

Messi's disappointment after missing the Champions League final consumed him. "How could I miss a game like this? Some players wait ten years for a moment like this," he kept repeating. The frustration of an 18-year-old who had pushed his body too far and paid the price weighed heavily on him.

A fellow player saw it differently. "It wasn't childish—it was the reaction of someone who understood how rare these moments are." Others struggled to understand. "Your team has just won, you're 18, you're going to the World Cup… why react like this?" For Messi, missing the game wasn't just a setback—it was a painful lesson in patience.

One of the players, sensing his sadness, draped his medal around Messi's neck. "One day, you'll see how special this was." Slowly, the team's joy lifted him. His teammates carried the trophy to him, encouraging him to touch it, to feel part of the victory.

Years later, Messi reflected: "I should have enjoyed it more. I was too caught up in my disappointment. Now I understand how special that night was."

The Hat-Trick That Changed Everything

After a painful Champions League exit against Liverpool, Barcelona looked to regain momentum in El Clásico against Real Madrid on March 10, 2007. The game became a defining moment in Messi's career, marking his transition from promising talent to leader.

Messi, still sporting his long hair, stepped up as Ronaldinho's influence faded.

With a struggling striker and a defender sent off before halftime, the teenager took charge. He tormented the opposition's right-back, creating space and waiting for the right moment. When a veteran striker put the opposing team ahead, Messi responded by slotting home from the left after receiving a pass from the struggling striker. Underneath his jersey, he revealed a message: Fuerza, tío—a tribute to his uncle.

The opposition regained the lead through a penalty, but Messi struck again, capitalizing on a combination play to level the score at 2-2. The match remained relentless, and when a defender put the opposition ahead for the third time, it seemed the home team would fall short.

Then, in stoppage time, Messi received the ball under pressure. With his first touch, he cut inside, evading a desperate lunge. "I found myself one-on-one with the goalkeeper," he later recalled. A precise left-footed shot found the bottom corner. The stadium erupted.

He kissed the badge repeatedly. "The team gave me everything," he explained afterward. His teammates swarmed him, and as a teammate later recalled, they celebrated without words—just raw emotion. Typically the main figure in these clashes, the striker acknowledged Messi's rise: "Today, he is above any other player. He has an extra gear."

Another player, recalling the game years later, joked, "Without my run down the right, he wouldn't have had as much space for that third goal." But everyone knew: this was the teenager's night.

Laporta recognized the significance: "Great players shine in big matches. Messi never hides—especially against Real Madrid." Seven goals in his first eight Clásicos cemented his status. By 2013, he had matched the legendary Argentinian footballer, Alfredo Di Stéfano's record of 18 goals in the fixture.

That night, Messi had erased the pain of missing the Champions League final and the World Cup. He was now the player Barcelona looked to. The Messi era had begun.

A Goal for the Ages

By March 2007, Barcelona acknowledged Messi's growing impact with a new seven-year contract. His earnings soared, reflecting his transformation from a rising star to a player capable of deciding games single-handedly. But while financial figures highlighted his value off the pitch, it was what happened on it that truly defined him.

In the Copa del Rey semi-final against Getafe, Messi scored a goal that would be remembered forever. It was the 29th minute, and he received the ball near the halfway line. With his first touch, he skipped past one defender, then another. He feinted left, nutmegged his next opponent, and accelerated. Two more defenders closed in, but he slid between them, his movement so precise it seemed inevitable. Now, only the goalkeeper stood in his way. He glided past him, almost losing control, but recovered just in time to lift the ball over a desperate defender and into the net.

It took twelve seconds, seventy yards, and thirteen touches. The entire stadium erupted. The comparisons to Maradona's legendary 1986 World Cup goal against England were instant. Those on the pitch were left speechless. Teammates grabbed their heads in disbelief, while the Getafe players stood frozen, aware they had just been part of history.

In the dressing room, the excitement lingered. Some told him outright: That was Maradona's goal! But Messi himself was indifferent. He hadn't planned it. He never did. It simply happened. While others marveled, he shrugged it off as just another goal.

The press exploded with headlines drawing parallels between him and Maradona. Calls from Argentina poured in, stirring up national pride. But Messi, true to his nature, remained unmoved. He didn't boast, didn't replay the moment over and over. He simply smiled when his teammates reenacted it, imitating commentators shouting in disbelief.

It was a goal that changed perceptions. Until then, Messi was seen as a prodigious talent, but that night, people realized he was something more. He had done it against senior professionals, not in training or youth matches. Could Barcelona move on from Ronaldinho? The whispers began.

Messi didn't see it as the moment he arrived. But for the world, it was undeniable: a new era had begun.

Even as the football world celebrated, it was clear that such a goal would never be repeated. Defenders became more vigilant, tracking his every movement, and Barcelona recognized that relying on solo brilliance was not a sustainable strategy.

Rijkaard later gave Messi what he considered his best piece of advice: "Finish the play: shoot or play the final ball but don't carry on dribbling."

He warned Messi against exhausting himself by constantly seeking to weave through entire defences. Instead, he encouraged him to conserve his energy and focus on making decisive contributions in the final third. Manager Guardiola, too, would later analyze that goal as a tactical flaw, highlighting how it stemmed from Barcelona's deeper issues—too much individual effort, poor team positioning, and a lack of cohesion in attack.

Messi himself had been looking for a teammate. That evening, over dinner with his father, he repeatedly said, "I was looking for Eto'o to pass him the ball." But the opportunity never arose, and instinct took over.

Rijkaard assumed the tie was settled and left Messi out for the return leg. It was a grave miscalculation. Barcelona collapsed in Madrid, losing 4–0 to Getafe and suffering one of the most humiliating eliminations in the club's history.

The focus shifted to the league title. Barcelona controlled their own fate, but in the final stretch, defensive lapses cost them dearly. Espanyol's player struck a late equalizer at the Camp Nou, and Real Madrid, level on points, edged them out on goal difference. It was a devastating end to the season.

That night, Messi learned a crucial lesson. After scoring both goals in the 2–2 draw against Espanyol, including one with his hand—a move eerily reminiscent of Maradona's infamous Hand of God—he saw how thin the line was between triumph and regret. While South American football culture often embraced such cunning, Messi felt differently. He never repeated the act.

Losing the league in such a manner reinforced his evolving mentality. He realized that individual brilliance alone wasn't enough. The best way to win was to play within the team.

CHAPTER 9
BATTLING FOR GREATNESS

Football Nights

At the Champions League semifinals, Barcelona delivered a footballing masterclass against Bayern Munich. They dismantled the German side 4-0 in a first half that left no doubt about their dominance.

Messi led the charge, scoring twice and assisting another, showcasing his ability to dictate the biggest games. His opening goal, a quick one-two with Eto'o, set the tone, and within minutes, he returned the favor, assisting the Cameroonian for the second. Before halftime, Messi latched onto a Henry cross for his second, and Henry himself added a fourth after a dazzling display of attacking fluidity.

The stadium erupted when Messi seemed to have won a penalty, only for the referee to book him for simulation, a decision that left fans furious and even saw Guardiola sent off in protest. But nothing could dampen the brilliance of Barcelona's performance.

Messi's numbers were staggering—two goals, two assists, three shots on target, and one against the woodwork. With eight goals in eight Champions League matches, he was already Europe's top scorer. It was called the 'best forty-five minutes in the history of the club.' It was a statement of intent, yet one that would soon be surpassed.

Barcelona's 6-2 demolition of Real Madrid at the Bernabéu was a turning point in the club's modern history. Guardiola made a crucial tactical shift, moving Messi from his usual right-wing position into a central false nine role. The decision exploited the weaknesses of Madrid's center-backs, forcing them to step up and leaving gaps for others to exploit. Messi thrived in this free role, linking with others in midfield and orchestrating every attacking move.

Madrid took an early lead, but Barcelona responded quickly.

Messi's delicate chip over the defense set up a forward for the equalizer, and soon after, a defender put the team ahead with a header. Messi himself got on the scoresheet before halftime, slotting home after a brilliant one-two. Though a defender briefly reignited the opposition's hopes in the second half, Messi, Xavi, and Iniesta soon completed the rout.

The dressing room was euphoric. Players who hadn't featured in the game celebrated as if they had, understanding the magnitude of what had just happened. Silvinho described it as "ninety minutes of perfect football." Guardiola, beaming in the press conference, summed it up: "Those three can make any idea a good one."

This was not just a victory—it was a declaration. Barcelona had conquered Madrid on their own turf with style, intelligence, and overwhelming superiority. The tactical experiment was shelved for the time being, but Guardiola had found a weapon that he would later unleash on an even grander stage. Sir Alex Ferguson would soon discover that the Barcelona he thought he was preparing for was no longer the same.

The Road to Rome

Barcelona's path to the Champions League final was defined by resilience and brilliance. After a tense first leg against opponents at the Camp Nou ended in a goalless draw, the second leg at an opponent's stadium proved to be even more challenging. An early strike put the Catalans on the back foot, and the task became even harder when a defender was sent off in the 66th minute. Yet, even with ten men, Barcelona refused to surrender. The opposing coach's decision to replace a forward with a defender signaled that the opposition was content to defend, a move that only emboldened Barcelona. Deep into stoppage time, Messi provided the crucial assist, setting up a midfielder for a stunning goal that silenced the opposition's stadium and sent Barcelona to the final in a European city.

Before that, there was the Copa del Rey final against Athletic Bilbao. Messi, playing in his first final as a starter, was instrumental in Barcelona's emphatic 4-1 victory. Athletic had taken the lead, but Barcelona responded in devastating fashion. Leo, at the heart of almost every attacking move, scored the second goal with a display of precision and patience, dribbling in a crowded box before finding the gap to fire past the keeper. Three days later, Barcelona became league champions without kicking a ball, as Real Madrid's loss confirmed their title. With the domestic double secured, one challenge remained—Manchester United in the Champions League final.

The media framed the match as a battle between the two best players in the world—Messi and Cristiano Ronaldo. Ferguson's United were labeled the favorites, and much of the buildup revolved around their contrasting styles. While their rivalry would be exaggerated over the years, on the pitch, there was always mutual respect. Messi, however, had his own personal challenge—he had yet to score against an English team.

In the days leading up to the final, Guardiola tested a tactical shift—playing Messi as a false nine rather than on the wing. The reasoning was simple: United's center-backs were dominant in the air but hesitant to step forward. By pulling them out of position, Messi could exploit the space and disrupt United's defensive structure.

On the eve of the final, as the squad settled into their hotel, Messi's only concern wasn't tactics or nerves—it was that his room didn't have a bed. A quick call resolved the issue, and with that, Leo returned to his usual pre-game calm. Walking through the corridors of the team hotel, he held his match ticket in his hand as if it were any other day. He was ready.

Treble Night

The Champions League final in Rome was a defining moment in Leo Messi's career. With Barcelona's 2-0 victory over Manchester United, the world could no longer deny what his teammates had already known—Messi was the best player in the world. He finished the tournament as the top scorer with nine goals, two ahead of his closest rivals, and had cemented himself as the heir to football's throne.

On the pitch, the celebrations were euphoric, but for some, the night carried a deeper meaning. Silvinho, who had played his final game for Barcelona, embraced Messi with an intensity the younger man did not yet understand. It was a silent farewell, an acknowledgment that their journey together had reached its end. Years later, when Silvinho sent Messi a photo of their embrace, the memory finally clicked. "You don't remember, do you?" Silvinho asked. "Yes, I do," Leo replied, finally grasping the significance of that emotional moment.

After the match, Barcelona had arranged a celebration in a Roman castle, but the night turned chaotic. What was meant to be a private gathering turned into a free-for-all, with players struggling to find space to enjoy their historic triumph with their families. Messi, always uncomfortable with excessive attention off the pitch, found himself lost in the crowd. The moment, meant for celebration, felt suffocating instead.

The mood lightened the next morning on the flight back to Barcelona.

Still buzzing from the victory, Messi grabbed the microphone and entertained his teammates with his sharp Argentinian humor, a rare moment of unguarded joy.

Later that evening, standing at the Camp Nou in front of thousands of adoring fans, Messi—wrapped in a Catalan scarf and cap, his voice hoarse from the night before—shouted, "Next year we are going to carry on and win everything, and we are going to celebrate it all over again. ¡Visca el Barça i visca Catalunya!"

His father, Jorge, watched the scene unfold with a mix of pride and embarrassment. This was the son he had raised—a footballing genius who let his performances speak for him, but who, in moments of triumph, still surprised even those closest to him.

Messi's Ascent and the Changing of the Guard

With 38 goals across all competitions, Lionel Messi had officially taken his place as the focal point of Barcelona's attack. Thierry Henry and Samuel Eto'o had also been prolific, but Guardiola saw the future— Messi would play centrally, and the team would be built around him. However, this vision required changes.

Samuel Eto'o, who had been instrumental in the team's success, found himself at odds with Guardiola. The Cameroonian striker, fierce and unyielding, was unwilling to continually adapt his game for Messi's development. He challenged Guardiola's authority in training, reminding him that a former midfielder could never understand the instincts of a striker. The relationship fractured beyond repair. Guardiola, appreciative of Eto'o's contributions, saw no path forward. The club sought a replacement, ultimately securing Zlatan Ibrahimović in a complex and costly deal. Eto'o was included as part of the transfer, heading to Inter Milan, where he would soon find success.

Guardiola's tactical shift was designed to maximize Messi's impact. With Ibrahimović playing as a traditional forward, Barcelona could stretch defenses, allowing Messi to drift inside and exploit space. It was a move reminiscent of the classic Dutch 4-3-3 system, with a strong center-forward capable of holding up the ball. However, chemistry was crucial, particularly between Messi and Ibrahimović. The season's first true test of this new approach came in December, at the FIFA Club World Cup in Abu Dhabi.

Messi entered the tournament carrying a minor ankle injury, working with his trainer to regain fitness. He was benched for the semi-final against Atlante, a match that unexpectedly became a struggle when the Mexican side scored in the fourth minute. Barcelona found an equalizer, but the game remained tense. In the 54th minute, Messi was introduced. Within moments, Ibrahimović set him up for the go-ahead goal.

Before the final against Estudiantes de la Plata, Guardiola delivered a speech that would be remembered for years: "If we lose today, we will still be the best team in the world. If we win, we will be eternal."

But the match did not unfold as expected. Estudiantes struck first, forcing Barcelona to fight for their legacy.

Messi's Defining Moment in Abu Dhabi

The final of the FIFA Club World Cup in Abu Dhabi was supposed to be a formality for Guardiola's Barcelona. They had already won everything in 2009—La Liga, the Copa del Rey, the Champions League, the Spanish Super Cup, and the European Super Cup. One more title would complete an unprecedented six-trophy haul. But Estudiantes de la Plata, led by Juan Sebastián Verón, had other ideas. They were tough, disciplined, and determined not to be another victim of Barcelona's brilliance.

When Mauro Boselli scored in the 37th minute, Barcelona were in trouble. The Argentine striker rose above the defense and headed past Valdés, giving the underdogs a lead they fiercely defended. The game became an exercise in frustration. Barcelona dominated possession, but the usual fluency was missing. Guardiola's side kept probing, Messi drifting inside from the right, Henry and Ibrahimović searching for space. But Estudiantes held firm, resisting wave after wave of Barcelona's attacks.

With the clock running down, Guardiola turned to his bench. Players were replaced at halftime, adding more dynamism in attack. But time was slipping away. As the match entered its final minute, Barcelona were on the verge of defeat. Then, Pedro, the man who had already scored in every competition that year, arose.

The game went to extra time, and in the 110th minute, Messi delivered the final blow. The ball deflected into his path inside the box, a chance that would normally require a header. But instead of using his head, Messi chested the ball into the net past the goalkeeper. It was instinctive, precise, and decisive. Barcelona had done it—six titles in one year. No team had ever achieved such dominance before.

As the final whistle blew, Guardiola broke down in tears. It was the culmination of everything he had worked for, a perfect end to a perfect year. Messi was the first to embrace him, sharing in the overwhelming emotion of the moment.

After the match, Messi spoke with his usual humility. "A lot of time is going to have to pass for us to realize what we have achieved," he said. "It's going to be very difficult for anyone to repeat it because no other side has ever managed it."

The celebrations that followed were as memorable as the match itself. In the dressing room, the players took photos with the trophy, reveling in their achievement. Yet, even in these moments of triumph, the team's dynamics were shifting. Ibrahimović, the big summer signing, remained somewhat detached from the group, celebrating with his own circle. Messi, in contrast, was right at the heart of it all, alongside Xavi, Puyol, and Iniesta.

At just 22 years old, Messi had completed football's most perfect season. He had won every major trophy, finished as the Champions League's top scorer, and was now the undisputed focal point of Barcelona's attack. He had gone from a prodigious talent to the best player in the world, and he wasn't done yet.

CHAPTER 10
THE DEFINING ERA

The Guardiola Effect

As Messi's influence grew, so did his importance to the club. In just over a year, he signed two new contracts, each reflecting his rising stature. His salary increased significantly, with bonuses tied to performance and team success. His release clause, already astronomical, climbed even higher, ensuring he remained the club's most valuable asset.

Following a historic year, the team took a well-earned break, but Messi's return to action was carefully managed. Guardiola, always mindful of his squad's fitness, opted to rest him for a league match, focusing on an upcoming cup tie. Messi, eager to play, made himself available, but the coach stood firm. Without him, the team struggled to break down a deep defensive line, suffering an early setback.

The disappointment was evident, and Guardiola, recognizing his squad's hunger, adjusted his approach. For the second leg, he fielded the strongest lineup possible, determined to reignite their competitive fire.

For the first time under Guardiola, Barcelona faced elimination in a knockout match. The rain poured relentlessly, adding drama to a relentless second half filled with near misses. Messi, always a fierce competitor, was overcome with frustration. He hid his face in his shirt, silently processing the loss. Most of his teammates understood—this was his way of dealing with disappointment. No words were needed. His fire burned quietly, ready to reignite for the battles ahead.

Messi's evolution as a footballer reached a critical turning point during the second season under Guardiola. Despite his growing influence on the pitch, there were moments of struggle—matches where he was not as involved, games where his positioning limited his effectiveness. Guardiola, ever the meticulous tactician, refused to blame the player. Instead, he saw it as his own failure to maximize Messi's potential.

A key moment came during a Champions League match in Germany. Messi, positioned on the wing, was unable to influence the game as he had before. He cut inside frequently, searching for the ball, but in doing so, left his flank exposed. The opposition exploited this weakness, pushing forward with ease. Afterward, Guardiola analyzed every aspect of the game, recognizing that the issue wasn't Messi's ability—it was where he was being asked to play.

For years, he had started out wide, using his dribbling to cut inside and attack. But now, with another forward occupying the center, his natural game was disrupted. More importantly, it disrupted the team. The traditional 4-3-3 setup, which had worked so well, was suddenly causing congestion in attack. There was no longer enough space for Messi to operate as he wanted, and defensively, the team suffered.

Guardiola didn't need to be told directly, but he could see it clearly— Messi needed to move centrally. He began preparing the shift, waiting for the right moment to implement the change permanently. The player, too, knew that something had to change. His instincts had already been leading him toward the center of the pitch, and now, the manager was ready to make that movement official.

The conversation between them was brief but decisive. Messi was direct—he felt restricted, unable to influence the game as much as he wanted. Guardiola reassured him that adjustments would be made. From then on, the transformation was inevitable. The team would be built around Messi in his most natural role, with everything structured to allow him maximum influence.

This change marked the beginning of an unstoppable rise. With the tactical evolution complete, Messi was about to reach a level never seen before in modern football.

Messi's Tactical Evolution:
The Birth of the False Nine

By 2010, Leo Messi had already cemented himself as a crucial figure in his team, but Guardiola saw an even greater potential waiting to be unleashed. He believed Messi could be most effective when surrounded by a structured, disciplined unit—one that provided him with stability while allowing him the creative freedom to destabilize opponents. Messi was to be the unpredictable element, but in order for that to work, his teammates had to function with absolute precision.

Guardiola made the bold decision to shift Messi permanently into a central role. He explained to him directly: "From now on, you will play through the middle. You're going to score three or four goals per game." The transformation was immediate. Four days after struggling in Germany, Messi played as a central attacker in the return leg at home, leading his team to a dominant 4–0 victory, scoring twice and setting up another. In three matches, he had scored seven goals. His dip in form was over, and his goal tally skyrocketed.

The shift was not purely tactical; it was also the result of Messi's own evolution. He had begun drifting inward from the right, seeking more involvement. Guardiola simply formalized what was already happening.

Years later, in an interview, the coach reflected: "Leo understood what playing through the middle meant very quickly. Would I have done it without him? Maybe not."

With Messi at the heart of the attack, the team adapted to his rhythm. Pressing became more effective because everyone knew where Messi would be. He had complete freedom, but the players around him followed strict positioning rules to support his movement. This allowed for quicker transitions and a more coordinated effort to recover possession.

However, not everyone fit into this new system. A particular moment in London highlighted the growing divide between Messi and a teammate. During an intense match, the Swedish striker was isolated up front, struggling to link up with the team's play. Yet, he managed to score twice, giving the team a brief advantage. Despite this, Messi remained largely uninvolved, prompting sharp words from two midfield generals. They demanded more from him—more energy, more involvement. Messi took their criticism seriously, acknowledging their importance in his development.

Off the pitch, Messi's closest allies ensured he remained protected. A group of teammates, including a veteran defender and an energetic right-back, acted as his enforcers. If anyone dared to foul Messi in training, they would step in immediately. The camaraderie in the dressing room was strong, built on mutual respect and the shared goal of making Messi the best player in the world.

The return leg against Arsenal loomed, and Messi knew he had underperformed in the first encounter. He had listened to his teammates, taken their criticism to heart. The time had come to deliver a performance that would define his new role—and silence any doubts about who the team truly revolved around.

Throughout that season of tactical adjustments, Messi notched three hat-tricks before his standout performance against Arsenal.

Spain hailed Messi's performance as otherworldly, with headlines declaring his four-goal display had single-handedly dismantled Arsenal and secured Barcelona's place in the semi-finals. Spanish media praised his ability to redefine the sport, placing him among the legends who had previously scored four goals in a Champions League match.

In England, the reaction was one of admiration and resignation. The British press acknowledged that any lingering debates about the best player of the generation had been settled that night. Analysts described the performance as one of the greatest ever seen in European competition, with Messi's technical brilliance and composure leaving Arsenal powerless.

In Italy, football commentators compared Messi's performance to the dominance of past greats, emphasizing how rare it was to witness such mastery. France and Germany also highlighted his individual brilliance, reinforcing the notion that he was in a league of his own.

After the match against Arsenal, Leo held onto the ball as a keepsake—a personal trophy from that unforgettable night. It wasn't out of superstition, unlike some strikers who believe such mementos bring luck to their careers and homes. Superstitions held no place in his routine, nor did he seek them. When asked about it on UEFA's website, he simply stated, "No, I don't have any superstitions. Before playing, I only think about my family."

Winning the Ballon d'Or

The 2009 Ballon d'Or was awarded in emphatic fashion, with a near-unanimous vote recognizing the brilliance of a player who had dominated European football throughout the year. His performances for his club, leading them to an unprecedented treble, left little room for debate. By the end of the season, he had established himself as the best player in the world, surpassing his closest rival by a record margin in the voting.

Winning the Ballon d'Or required an exceptional blend of individual brilliance and team success. The award, historically given to the best footballer in the world, was heavily influenced by performances in domestic leagues, continental tournaments, and international competitions. Consistency was crucial—players who maintained top form throughout the year, delivering goals, assists, and game-changing moments, stood the best chance.

A key factor in securing the prize was excelling in high-stakes matches. Champions League performances often carried significant weight, as did standout displays in title-deciding league matches or major international tournaments. Voters, comprised of journalists worldwide, tended to favor players who led their teams to trophies while demonstrating skill, leadership, and influence.

Tactical adaptability and versatility could also set a player apart. Those who dominated multiple positions or contributed beyond scoring— through playmaking, pressing, or defensive work—gained favor. Ultimately, winning the Ballon d'Or was about combining personal excellence with collective triumph.

Messi's journey to the award was defined by his role in his team's success. He was the top scorer in the Champions League, netting nine times, including a crucial goal in the final. His influence was undeniable as his team secured the league title and the domestic cup, completing a historic treble. With a total of 38 goals across all competitions, his goal-scoring prowess was matched only by his ability to create chances and dictate the rhythm of the game.

What set him apart was not just the statistics but his performances in decisive moments. In the Champions League knockout stages, he produced mesmerizing displays, scoring four goals against an English side in the quarter-finals. His agility, close control, and acceleration allowed him to navigate through defenders effortlessly, making him nearly unstoppable. His goal in the final, a perfectly placed header, was a moment that cemented his status as the most dominant force in football.

The impact of his success was reflected in the Ballon d'Or voting. He received 473 points out of a possible 480, a staggering 240 points ahead of the previous winner. His closest challengers were his teammates, whose contributions were also recognized, but his influence was on another level. His club's style of play, built around possession and quick passing, allowed him to flourish, and his chemistry with the midfielders behind him elevated his game even further.

This award was not just about one exceptional season—it was a culmination of years of progress. Since breaking into the first team, he had been steadily improving, learning from the best, and refining his game. By 2009, he had developed into a complete forward, capable of playing multiple roles in attack. He had the skill and intelligence to operate as a playmaker, the speed to play on the wing, and the finishing ability of a pure striker.

The recognition went beyond the Ballon d'Or. His performances in 2009 solidified his position as the face of the sport. His club rewarded him with a contract extension, making him the highest-paid player in their history, and his influence in the team continued to grow. The question was no longer whether he was the best player in the world but rather how long he would stay at the top.

With this triumph, he became the first from his country to win the award under its revised rules. He paid tribute to his coach, acknowledging the impact of a system that allowed him to thrive. More importantly, he viewed this achievement as the beginning, not the peak, of his career. As he lifted the trophy, the football world knew that this was only the first of many.

Best Footballer Ever?

"At 23, Messi is the best of the best."

The Champions League final at Wembley was the stage for a performance that cemented Messi's place among football's greatest. Facing an opponent determined to avoid the mistakes of two years earlier, he delivered a masterclass of precision, intelligence, and dominance. From the outset, he dictated the rhythm, linking up with teammates, finding space where none existed, and controlling the game with an effortless brilliance that left Manchester United chasing shadows.

When the English side took the field, they had a plan. Their coach had spoken about learning from previous encounters, about knowing how to stop the flow of Barcelona's play. Yet, within minutes, it became clear that no amount of preparation could neutralize what they were facing. With quick exchanges, relentless movement, and an understanding built through years of playing together, Barcelona overwhelmed their opponents. The midfield trio behind Messi provided the foundation, but it was the Argentinian's movement, shifting between roles, that made it impossible for Manchester United to find their footing.

The match changed when he found the net. Cutting inside from his favored position, he saw the space, recognized the hesitation of the goalkeeper, and unleashed a strike from outside the box. It was not the most spectacular goal of his career, but it was the most decisive. As the ball hit the net, he celebrated with unrestrained emotion, kicking an advertising board and nearly jumping into the crowd. It was the goal that broke the game open, the goal that ensured there would be no comeback.

For the remainder of the match, he orchestrated everything. The statistics told the story—possession overwhelmingly in favor of his team, more than twenty attempts on goal, while their opponents managed only four. When the final whistle blew, the celebrations began. His coach, the man who had built a team around his talents, embraced him and whispered words of gratitude. In the press conference that followed, there was no hesitation in his verdict: "He's the best player I've seen and will ever see."

The victory was more than just another Champions League triumph—it was a statement. The performance left no doubt about who was the best player in the world. Opponents had tried pressing high, they had tried dropping deep, they had tried physicality. None of it worked. His ability to adapt, to find solutions in the midst of defensive walls, had no equal.

Even as the celebrations continued, thoughts turned to the future. He would not allow himself to become complacent. As he lifted the trophy, he spoke of winning more, of continuing to improve. There was no arrogance, no sense of arrival—only the hunger to keep going.

After Wembley, the challenge shifted to the national team. Returning to Argentina, he faced pressure unlike anything he had encountered in club football. Despite scoring 53 goals that season, criticism was fierce. He had not scored for his country in more than two years. Comparisons with past legends resurfaced, and doubts over his ability to lead Argentina became louder. The disappointment of the Copa América, the scrutiny of every performance, and the expectations of an entire nation weighed heavily.

When the national team changed coaches, his new manager sought advice on how best to handle him. The answer was simple: don't try to change him. Let him play in his way, give him the right teammates, and most importantly, never substitute him—not even for a standing ovation.

Back at his club, he returned to a team that had been strengthened. New signings arrived, a rival manager added fuel to an already intense battle, and the next season promised to be even more challenging. But as always, his response would come on the pitch.

CHAPTER 11
RECORD BREAKER

The Clásico Wars

As the 2010–11 season began, optimism ran high. Several players had departed, including key figures in midfield and attack, but the club had reinforced its squad with the arrival of new talent. With Barcelona now widely regarded as the best team in the world and its star forward as the greatest player of his generation, the challenge was to stay ahead of rivals who were determined to find ways to neutralize their dominance.

Messi entered the season with a mix of determination and frustration, still carrying the disappointment of Argentina's World Cup exit in the quarter-finals against the hosts, Germany. But he had formed a strong bond during the tournament with a compatriot who was eager to join him in Spain. Javier Mascherano was a tenacious midfielder who had spent the summer pressing Leo to put in a word with his coach, knowing that the club was searching for a replacement in his position. "Tell him I'm not one of those bad Argentines," he joked, hoping to convince the manager that he would be the right fit.

Messi's influence extended beyond the pitch. His recommendation carried weight, and soon enough, Javier's move to Barcelona was finalized. When he arrived, he was welcomed with the usual formalities—photos, press conferences, the unveiling at Camp Nou. But what mattered most was the personal moment that followed. Away from the cameras, in a quiet room reserved for family members after matches, Leo greeted him with a simple embrace and a single word: "Welcome."

On the pitch, Javier quickly understood what made the team so effective. The game revolved around Leo—not just his skill but his ability to read play, adapt to situations, and dictate the tempo. He wasn't just a goalscorer; he was an orchestrator, capable of shifting the rhythm of a match in an instant. Those around him, from midfield to attack, knew instinctively where to move.

By now, words were hardly needed. His connection with teammates was almost telepathic, particularly with those who had played alongside him for years. Everything functioned seamlessly, each movement anticipating the next. "There are moments when I can go an entire match without saying a word to him," admitted one of his closest partners on the field. The team operated with a precision that seemed effortless, but it was the product of years of familiarity and an unparalleled understanding of the game.

Messi's Moment

With the league title nearly secured, the first of four Clásicos in quick succession arrived at the Bernabéu. The match was a tense prelude to the battles ahead, with both teams knowing that the upcoming encounters—especially in the Champions League—would define their seasons. Madrid, led by a coach intent on psychological warfare, set the tone with a tactical approach designed to suffocate Messi's influence. The grass was left uncut, the pitch dry, and an extra defender was deployed in midfield to clog the spaces Leo operated in. The result was a physical, aggressive contest, filled with fouls, penalties, and animosity.

Madrid fans hurled insults at Leo every time he touched the ball, and a laser was even pointed at his face as he prepared to take a penalty. But he remained composed, converting the spot-kick with precision. Frustrations boiled over in the final moments when he chased down a loose ball, barely missing it, then instinctively struck it into the stands, narrowly avoiding a few bystanders. It was an unusual display of emotion, a rare moment where his frustration escaped into the open. The psychological battle was heating up, and Madrid's approach was working—Barcelona looked rattled.

The Copa del Rey final followed, and despite Barcelona's dominance in possession, Madrid's tactical discipline stifled their attack. Once again, Messi found himself up against an aggressive defensive block, with his usual diagonal runs cut off by the extra midfielder. It was a game of patience, waiting for an opening that never came. A single counter-attack decided the final, leaving Barcelona devastated. Leo took it personally, feeling that he hadn't done enough, that he hadn't found the breakthrough. His frustration was doubled when he realized that Madrid had found a system that could work against him.

The Champions League semi-final became a battle of contrasting philosophies. Madrid aimed to disrupt and destroy; Barcelona sought to control and create. The tension escalated beyond the pitch. At the pre-match press conference, Guardiola took a direct shot at his rival, calling him "the fucking boss" of the media mind games. The real contest, he said, would take place on the field.

In the first leg, Madrid pressed aggressively but without taking risks. Their defensive anchor, deployed specifically to stop Messi, was crucial to their structure. But in a moment of recklessness, he lunged at an opponent with his studs showing. The challenge was exaggerated, but the referee's decision was final: a red card. Moments later, Madrid's manager was also dismissed. The match had reached a boiling point, and someone needed to take control.

Messi stepped up. In the space of a few minutes, he dismantled Madrid's defense with two breathtaking goals. The second, a mesmerizing solo effort, left defenders trailing in his wake before he slotted the ball past the goalkeeper. It was an exclamation point on a performance that cemented his status as the best in the world.

The return leg was played under protest from Madrid, who claimed Barcelona's players had exaggerated fouls to manipulate the referee. Messi stayed away from the off-field chaos, focusing solely on the task ahead. Madrid attempted a more aggressive approach, pressing higher, but it was too late. Barcelona controlled the match and booked their place in the final.

Guardiola praised Messi's ability to thrive in high-pressure situations. "He has the freedom to create because his teammates allow him to shine," he said. "This is what makes us a team."

Leo had emerged from the Clásico wars as the decisive factor, proving once again that when the stakes were highest, he delivered.

Overcoming Adversity: Messi's Struggles and Triumphs

Messi's journey was never just about his brilliance; it was about his ability to overcome adversity. In the relentless battles against Madrid, he endured targeted aggression, tactical obstacles, and psychological warfare. Every match against his greatest rivals became a war of attrition, testing his resilience as much as his skill.

During a particularly heated encounter, a moment of frustration escaped him—he spat near the opposing bench, provoking an immediate reaction. The coach on the other side made a dismissive gesture, branding him as "dirty." It was a rare lapse in Messi's composure, but it was also a reflection of the intensity he faced every time he stepped onto the pitch. Kicks to the ankles, late challenges, elbows—many of them went unseen. He was marked not just by defenders but by an entire tactical system designed to slow him down.

His tormentors took things even further. In a later league match, an opponent deliberately stepped on his hand while he was on the ground. The incident was dismissed as an accident, but the intent was clear. It was becoming harder to enjoy the game. The Clásicos had once been battles of skill, but under a new era of rivalry, they had become wars of attrition. Despite it all, Messi continued to shine, matching a legendary goalscoring record in these heated encounters. But cracks had started to appear in Barcelona's dominance, with other teams adopting the blueprint that had caused them problems.

Pressure from rivals wasn't just limited to the pitch. It extended into the media, the referees, and even the perception of Barcelona's success. A narrative emerged—people were growing tired of their dominance. Even within his own team, celebrations were laced with tension. After one particular victory, a mid-flight celebration turned chaotic when Messi, unknowingly, triggered an emergency door mechanism. The laughter that followed masked the reality of a draining and difficult season.

The challenges didn't stop. Opponents found new ways to limit his influence, crowding the midfield, cutting off his space, and forcing him into physical duels. The constant harassment was taking a toll. Yet, Messi adapted. He strengthened his body, working on his core and lower body to absorb the constant impacts. His physical transformation was noticed by everyone—his legs more defined, his balance unshakable. He was no longer pushed off the ball as easily, no longer bullied into submission.

Defenders studied him obsessively, but stopping him was another matter entirely. Time and again, he would execute the same move—drifting from the right, cutting inside, shifting through gaps that seemed non-existent, and curling a shot into the far corner. It was predictable, yet unstoppable. "Even if you think you know what he's going to do, he's so quick and his timing so good that it becomes almost impossible to stop," admitted one of his opponents.

For Messi, overcoming challenges wasn't about avoiding them—it was about adapting. Every obstacle became another step in his evolution. Whether it was tactical restrictions, physical punishment, or psychological warfare, he never stopped moving forward. And as long as he had the ball at his feet, he always found a way.

Masterclass at Wembley

The final in London was a demonstration of absolute superiority, with Messi at the heart of it. From the first whistle, he roamed freely, combining with teammates and searching for openings. His movement was relentless, dragging defenders out of position, creating space where none seemed to exist. Every touch carried intent, every pass dismantled defensive lines.

The opposition tried to stifle him, crowding the center, cutting off supply lines, but nothing worked. He adapted, drifting deep to collect the ball, linking up with midfield, then bursting forward when least expected. When the moment arrived, he struck with precision. A swift touch, a shift of balance, then a powerful shot from outside the box. The goalkeeper barely moved. The net rippled, and Messi exploded into celebration, punching the air, kicking an advertising board, overwhelmed by the magnitude of his own brilliance.

The game was played to the rhythm of his feet. He dictated the tempo, threading intricate passes, unlocking defensive walls. His influence extended beyond his own movements—his presence allowed those around him to flourish. When the team needed another goal, he played his part again, setting up the finish that sealed the triumph.

By the final whistle, it was clear—this was not just a victory; it was a statement. The opposition had spent months preparing, yet they were reduced to mere spectators, powerless against the force in front of them.

When the coach embraced Messi after the match, it was more than gratitude; it was acknowledgment. The player had made the system function, had elevated the game to an art form. That night, he was not just the best on the field—he was untouchable, on a level of his own.

As the season progressed, what had begun with optimism turned into a test of resilience. The team was rocked by devastating news—one coach diagnosed with cancer, a beloved teammate requiring a liver transplant, and in Messi's personal life, a family member also battling illness. The contrast between professional triumphs and personal grief became increasingly difficult to manage. Yet, Messi bore it in silence, keeping his emotions away from the training ground, using football as both an escape and a responsibility.

With the arrival of a new midfield dynamic, Messi's role evolved even further. He was no longer just a goal-scorer but a creator, a conductor in an orchestra built around his brilliance. His ability to dictate play from deep while still finishing attacks made him an unstoppable force. The Club World Cup final was another testament to his dominance, as he led his team to yet another trophy, solidifying his place as football's ultimate reference point.

During the tournament, he met a young Brazilian talent destined for greatness. Their conversation hinted at a future partnership, but Messi already knew that his club had secured the rising star. His influence extended beyond the pitch, as his foundation continued its work in supporting vulnerable children, a cause close to his heart.

As the year turned, Guardiola made a rare exception, granting Messi extra time with his family. He understood that behind the records, trophies, and accolades was a young man carrying burdens that no statistic could measure. When Messi returned, he shattered another record, becoming his club's all-time leading scorer at just 24. But some things remained the same—his pre-game nausea, the pressure, the weight of expectation. Through it all, he continued to rise.

The Night of Five Goals

The Champions League knockout stages demand brilliance. On a historic night, Messi delivered a performance that redefined the limits of individual excellence. His five-goal display against Bayer Leverkusen was not just a record-breaking feat but a masterclass in precision, composure, and sheer dominance.

From the opening whistle, he dictated the rhythm of the game, always a step ahead of the defenders. His first goal was a perfect example of his instinct and technique—a delicate chip over the goalkeeper, executed with effortless grace. As the match progressed, his influence grew stronger. Receiving a pass from Iniesta, he weaved through the defense and slotted home his second, making it clear that this was more than just another Champions League night.

The second half saw Messi at his most ruthless. A hat-trick arrived with another chip, this time off a pass. His fourth goal came from pure opportunism, capitalizing on a goalkeeper's fumble to tap it into the net. But it was his fifth that sealed the performance in history—a curling left-footed strike from outside the box, a goal of beauty and precision, one that left defenders and spectators in stunned admiration.

Bayer Leverkusen had no answer. Their defensive lines crumbled under the weight of Barcelona's relentless attack, orchestrated by Messi's movement, vision, and finishing. Every time he had the ball, the defenders hesitated, unsure whether to press or hold back, knowing that either decision could result in yet another moment of magic.

The numbers spoke for themselves. He had now scored 53 goals that season, a tally that seemed almost unreal. With his ability to operate as both a playmaker and a finisher, he had transformed his position, making it nearly impossible to mark him out of the game. The collective brilliance of his teammates provided the perfect structure, but it was Messi's execution that turned a dominant performance into a legendary one.

Messi's five-goal display in the Champions League left the footballing world in awe. His brilliance was undeniable, and those who witnessed it struggled to find words to describe his performance.

"Hurricane Messi," wrote a Spanish newspaper. "No one is more demanding than Messi himself, with each of his performances converted into a spectacle. The ball always arrives perfectly at the feet of the genius."

Messi himself reflected humbly: "I had the space, the goalie came out, and luckily it went in." But Opposing players and managers were equally stunned. Manchester United's Wayne Rooney declared, "Messi is unreal. For me, the best ever." Bayer's coach Robin Dutt summed it up: "Without Messi, Barcelona are the best team in the world. With him, they are from another galaxy."

CHAPTER 12
BATTLING FOR GREATNESS

Messi's Renewal

2012 ended with many defining moments for Messi—both on and off the pitch. On November 2, his first child, Thiago, was born, marking a new phase in his personal life. The announcement sent social media into a frenzy, not just because of the joyous news but also due to the time of birth—17:14—coinciding with a symbolic year in Catalan history.

Shortly after, Messi confirmed his long-term commitment to his club by signing a contract extension. His renewal was announced alongside two senior teammates, reinforcing a sense of unity within the dressing room. Behind the scenes, his father had turned down an astronomical offer from a Russian club willing to pay €400 million, a figure that would have made Messi the highest-paid player in history. Instead, he remained where he felt most at home, signing a deal until 2018 with a €250 million buyout clause.

Despite ongoing debates about tactical evolution, Barcelona continued their dominance in the league. Meanwhile, in Madrid, the cracks began to show, with mounting tensions disrupting their momentum. The footballing world watched as Messi entered a new era—balancing fatherhood, his peak years on the pitch, and an unwavering loyalty to his club.

By 2013, Messi had begun to embrace the realities of being a global icon, hiring a major advertising agency to manage his image. While his focus remained on football, the commercial side of his career grew rapidly, with his fashion choices becoming a subject of discussion. Dolce & Gabbana, a brand he frequently wore, played a role in refining his public persona. His bold choice of a polka-dot dinner suit at his fourth Ballon d'Or signaled a departure from his usual understated style, showing an evolving comfort with his celebrity status.

Beyond sponsorships and image management, Messi also faced more challenging aspects of fame. That summer, allegations of fiscal fraud surfaced, forcing him and his family into legal battles. As his star continued to rise, he had to navigate the pressures of being not just a footballer, but a global brand, learning to protect himself in a world beyond the pitch.

Battles

In 2013, Messi and his family found themselves at the center of a high-profile tax fraud investigation, a situation that quickly spiraled beyond the realm of football. The Spanish tax authorities had launched a crackdown on celebrities accused of tax evasion, aiming to restore public confidence during a time of economic hardship. Alongside other high-profile figures, Messi became a target, with the authorities seeking to make an example of him.

The issue stemmed from the management of his image rights, a common practice among elite footballers to minimize tax liabilities. Clubs often structure contracts to pay part of a player's earnings as salary and another portion as image rights, taxed at a lower rate through companies based in more favorable jurisdictions. In Messi's case, these payments were routed through offshore entities in Belize and Uruguay, which the authorities claimed were shell companies designed to evade taxes.

Messi, however, had little to no involvement in these financial decisions. His father, Jorge, had entrusted their financial affairs to an adviser who allegedly mismanaged the funds and attempted to withhold earnings from the family. When the Messis realized this, legal disputes arose between them and their adviser. Despite this, Spanish prosecutors maintained that Messi had ratified the fraudulent arrangements, implicating him in the case.

In an effort to resolve the issue, Messi and his father voluntarily paid €5 million—covering the alleged evaded taxes plus interest—and later an additional €10 million for subsequent years. Jorge Messi accepted full responsibility, stating that his son had no knowledge of financial dealings and was solely focused on football. However, the legal battle continued, with both Messi and his father summoned to court.

During his court appearance, Messi appeared visibly distressed, his discomfort evident as he testified. His father reiterated his full responsibility, emphasizing that Messi had no understanding of tax structures or financial operations. Despite the payments made, the case remained a significant moment in Messi's career, marking one of the few instances where his life outside of football took center stage in the public eye.

Though eventually settled, the controversy highlighted the

vulnerabilities of athletes who, despite their fame and fortune, often rely on financial advisers to handle complex legal and tax matters. The ordeal also reflected broader cultural differences in attitudes toward tax avoidance, with Spain's authorities attempting to send a message in a society where distrust of financial institutions and government corruption was prevalent.

For Messi, the experience was a harsh introduction to the realities of global fame. No longer just a footballer, he had become a figure whose every move—on and off the pitch—was scrutinized. The incident was a turning point, pushing him to be more cautious in his financial dealings.

Then, the day after one of his standout performances, Messi was sidelined with an injury.

A small tear in his right hamstring—a persistent issue throughout his career—forced him to step away from the game for weeks. These setbacks rarely happen by accident. The strain of constantly carrying his team, enduring relentless tackles, and playing through exhaustion had taken its toll.

For years, Messi had been an unstoppable force, defying physical limitations with his quick bursts of acceleration and sharp changes in direction. His body, however, had begun to protest. This was not the first time he had suffered from hamstring trouble, and it wouldn't be the last. Despite this, his determination never wavered. His goal was always the same: to recover as quickly as possible and return stronger.

During his absence, speculation swirled about the cause of his recurring injuries. Some pointed to his demanding schedule—playing almost every match for both club and country—while others believed he was pushing himself too hard. Medical staff carefully monitored his rehabilitation, structuring a two-phase recovery plan that saw him split his time between Barcelona and Buenos Aires. The club wanted to ensure he returned at full strength, but Messi's patience was wearing thin.

As he worked through his recovery, Barcelona continued their campaign without their talisman. The team adapted, but his absence was felt. He had already scored 14 goals that season, proving once again that he was the heartbeat of the squad. His return, however, needed to be managed carefully. There was a risk of aggravating the injury if he rushed back, yet Messi remained restless. He understood that football waited for no one, and every match he missed was another challenge to his dominance.

When he finally stepped back onto the pitch, there were no signs of hesitation. He moved with purpose, his signature dribbles as sharp as ever. The layoff had done little to dull his instincts. If anything, the time away had made him even more determined. His hunger to reclaim his place as the best player in the world burned brighter than before.

Another Star Begins to Shine

Barcelona welcomed a rising star to their ranks as Neymar arrived, bringing dazzling skill and immense potential. The Brazilian forward, already a sensation, now had the chance to play alongside the world's best, stepping into a team built around a singular genius.

The arrival of Neymar at Barcelona was meant to reinforce the team's attack, but it also introduced a delicate balancing act. For years, Messi had been the undisputed star, the focal point around whom everything revolved. But with Neymar's enormous media presence, his rising commercial value, and his hefty contract, Barcelona found themselves navigating an uneasy transition.

Messi had already welcomed the Brazilian with warmth, assuring him that he would be happy at the club. Their mutual respect on the pitch was undeniable, but off the field, the financial and political aspects of Neymar's signing created ripples. Despite Barcelona officially stating that Neymar's transfer cost €57 million, details soon emerged suggesting that commissions and bonuses for his father inflated the true figure. With those additional payments, Neymar was earning more than any other player at the club—including Messi himself.

This shift in financial hierarchy did not go unnoticed. It unsettled key figures in the squad. Three players left. A fourth renegotiated his contract. Even Cesc, already lower in the pecking order, entertained offers from Manchester United.

For Messi, these changes were not just financial; they affected the team's chemistry. He had built an instinctive connection with other players—footballers who understood his game on an almost subconscious level. Neymar, with his improvisational Brazilian style, brought flair but also unpredictability. Their partnership would take time to develop, and while their individual brilliance could shine in moments, the structural balance of the team was shifting.

Meanwhile, Messi continued his relentless pursuit of excellence. His status as Barcelona's leader on the pitch remained intact, but the landscape around him was evolving. For the first time, questions were being asked about whether the team should start looking beyond Messi for leadership. The press speculated about the emergence of a "new cockerel" in the dressing room, one that could eventually challenge Messi's position at the top of the hierarchy.

Despite all the noise surrounding Neymar's arrival, one truth remained: Messi was still the best player in the world. His influence was not just measured in goals and assists but in the way he carried the team through difficult moments. While Barcelona adjusted to the presence of a new superstar, Messi was determined to ensure that, on the pitch, his dominance remained unquestioned.

Barcelona's signing of Neymar was meant to reinforce the attack, but it inadvertently sparked an internal shift in power dynamics. To placate Messi, the club quickly moved to negotiate yet another contract renewal, barely six months after his last one. This ensured that, including bonuses, his earnings exceeded €20 million annually. However, the move was less about financial reward and more about reaffirming his status as the team's central figure.

The decision to bring in Neymar was both strategic and political. It strengthened Barcelona's squad but also ensured their rivals, particularly Madrid, couldn't sign him. Yet, the club seemed unprepared for the consequences of having two global superstars in the same team. With Guardiola gone and the European crown lost to Bayern, Barcelona faced a moment of transition. The club sought reinvention, but their method—bringing in a new star—raised more questions than answers.

Johan Cruyff foresaw the potential for conflict, drawing parallels to past instances where two dominant figures clashed. He suggested that selling Messi after securing Neymar might have been the best course of action. Others, including the former president, wondered how Messi would feel about a new star arriving with so much fanfare. While Neymar expressed admiration for Messi, the reality was that Barcelona had, whether intentionally or not, set up a situation where the two players might compete for dominance.

In the dressing room, questions were raised about how Neymar would fit in. Would he remain confined to the left wing for an entire season? Would the dynamics shift if he started overshadowing Messi? Senior players pondered what would happen if Neymar scored a hat-trick at

Camp Nou and the stadium erupted in celebration. The new manager would have to navigate the delicate balance between two massive talents.

Messi, for his part, maintained a diplomatic stance. Publicly, he welcomed Neymar, stating that he would bring strength to the team. But behind the scenes, there were likely frustrations. Messi had built his career at Barcelona, winning four Ballons d'Or, yet Neymar, unproven at the club, arrived as the highest-paid player at just 21. The unwritten rules of football dictated that such accolades and financial rewards should be earned, not simply handed out.

The media speculated about Messi's true feelings. Marca even questioned if Neymar's arrival would lead to conflicts similar to those with other players. Being number one came with a lot of pressure, after all. Messi was expected to deliver magic every game, and to do that, everything around him had to function smoothly. If it didn't, the blame fell on him first. That responsibility made him demanding—of his teammates and his club.

In their quest to find the perfect partner for their star, Barcelona had invested heavily in forwards, spending €205 million over five years. Yet, unlike the arrival of Ronaldinho, which revitalized the club, this was not about reigniting a golden era but rather reshaping a team that, at times, seemed to be running on autopilot. The challenge was clear: the number ten cared only about winning, and he would only accept players who could match his relentless drive.

New arrivals often arrived as direct competitors rather than as complementary figures, creating inevitable tension. The departure of a close friend and mentor like Tito Vilanova added to the emotional burden, and his struggles with recurring injuries further complicated matters. The fear among some was that Barcelona could repeat the mistakes of the past—allowing their brightest stars to rise, only to let them fall.

Then came Neymar's arrival on June 3, 2013. In a packed press conference, with 334 journalists in attendance, he addressed the inevitable comparisons and potential rivalry head-on:

"I am not bothered about being the leader of the team, nor of being the best player in the world. The best is here already and he is Messi. It is my good fortune and a tremendous honor to be able to play alongside him and to help him carry on being the best so he can win more Ballons d'Or."

CHAPTER 13
STRUGGLES AND HEARTBREAKS

The Germany Loss

"Nothing can console me."

Lionel Messi stood on the Maracanã podium with the Golden Ball in his hands, but his expression revealed nothing but disappointment. Despite being named the World Cup's most influential player, he knew Argentina had fallen short when it mattered most. The final against Germany had been within reach, yet a single moment of brilliance from the opposition had denied them glory.

The decision to award Messi the Golden Ball sparked debate, with even FIFA president Sepp Blatter expressing surprise. Diego Maradona, always outspoken, criticized the choice, suggesting it was more about marketing than merit. Messi himself dismissed the award's significance, stating that no personal accolade could ease the pain of losing the final.

The match had offered Argentina chances—Messi, Higuaín, and Palacio all had opportunities—but none converted. Where past legends had defined finals, Messi's moment never came. His dream of lifting the World Cup remained just that—a dream still unfulfilled.

The 2014 World Cup final was Lionel Messi's greatest opportunity to cement his legacy among football's immortals. With Argentina on the cusp of glory, he had the chance to join the ranks of Diego Maradona and Pelé as a World Cup-winning legend. However, fate had other plans. Argentina failed to capitalize on their chances, and an extra-time goal from a German player sealed their opponent team's victory.

Throughout the tournament, Messi had been instrumental in Argentina's success. He led his team with crucial goals in the group stage and played a key role in their knockout victories. But in the final, against a disciplined and relentless German side, Messi struggled to impose himself. Though he made some promising runs and nearly broke through the defense early in the match, his usual magic was missing. He managed just 66 touches, far below his usual influence, and his passing accuracy dropped to 70 percent—uncharacteristic numbers for a player of his caliber.

The defining moment came in the second half when Messi found himself with a golden chance. Played through on goal, he had only Manuel Neuer to beat. Millions watched in anticipation, expecting the clinical finish that had become his trademark. But instead of finding the net, his shot drifted agonizingly wide. It was a rare lapse, but one that proved decisive. Argentina had other chances, but in a match of fine margins, Messi's miss loomed largest.

Despite his disappointment, Messi was awarded the Golden Ball as the tournament's best player. The decision sparked controversy, with many—including Maradona—questioning whether he truly deserved it. Messi himself seemed indifferent to the honor, stating that no individual accolade could make up for the heartbreak of losing the final.

For Messi, the loss to Germany was a bitter reminder of how elusive the World Cup could be. Though he had carried Argentina to the final, he fell just short of football's ultimate prize. At 27, he knew he would have another chance, but the pain of Rio would linger as a defining moment in his career.

After Argentina's agonizing World Cup final defeat to Germany, Lionel Messi's words reflected the deep regret he and his teammates felt. "I don't know what to say, it's a pity," Messi said, reflecting on the chances his team had squandered. "I think we had the better chances in the game. For the rest of our lives we'll regret having those chances, and not being able to put them in." Messi's introspection revealed how deeply the missed opportunities haunted him and his teammates, especially in the biggest match of their careers.

Despite lifting the Golden Ball as the tournament's best player, Messi admitted that the trophy did little to console him. "I just wanted to win the World Cup. This award means nothing to me now," he declared after the final.

Messi also reflected on other key moments from the tournament, particularly the surprising 5-1 defeat of Spain by the Netherlands. "It was a game we were all looking forward to, with two great teams meeting," Messi said. He acknowledged the shock of seeing Germany's dominant 7-1 victory over Brazil in the semifinals, noting that it was a surprising result for everyone involved. Despite these unexpected outcomes, Messi and Argentina were focused solely on their own journey. "We did not expect Germany to be 3-0, 4-0 ahead so quickly. It was a huge surprise for everyone," he added.

Barcelona's New Chapter

The saga of Barcelona's MSN trio, composed of Lionel Messi, Luis Suarez, and Neymar, is one of football's most illustrious chapters.

It began in earnest in October 2014, when Suarez made his debut for the club following his transfer from Liverpool. In a move that had fans buzzing with excitement and anticipation, Barcelona announced the return of one of their own: Luis Enrique, as their new head coach. The former player and captain, who once graced the pitch at Camp Nou, was back to lead the team after a season of disappointment under Gerardo Martino.

FC Barcelona officially announced the appointment of Luis Enrique as their new head coach on a two-year contract. Enrique, a former Barcelona player who captained the team and later managed their B team, took over from Gerardo Martino after a season that saw Barca finish second in La Liga, just behind Atletico Madrid.

Enrique's return to Camp Nou followed a managerial tenure at Celta Vigo, where he impressed with his tactical acumen and ability to get the best out of his squad, guiding them to a respectable ninth-place finish in the league. His coaching career also included a stint at AS Roma, further enriching his experience and strategic approach to the game.

Known for his passionate and dynamic coaching style, Enrique was seen as a natural fit for Barcelona, aligning with the club's high standards and expectations for success. His deep connection with the club's philosophy and his previous success with the B team, where he achieved promotion to the Spanish second division, highlighted his capability to integrate young talents and implement a robust tactical system.

Barcelona's decision to bring Enrique on board reflected their commitment to revitalizing the team and aiming for dominance in both domestic and European competitions. His understanding of the club's culture and his proven track record made him a promising leader for the Catalans as they looked to reclaim their status at the top of Spanish and European football.

Messi, Suarez, and Neymar quickly established themselves as a formidable force, combining for an astonishing 364 goals during their time together, which spanned until 2017 when Neymar transferred to Paris Saint-Germain. Their synergy was immediate; in their first complete season together (2014-15), they amassed a total of 122 goals across all competitions, propelling Barcelona to a historic treble, clinching La Liga, the Copa del Rey, and the UEFA Champions League.

Their style was characterized by dazzling speed, pinpoint passes, and lethal finishing. Messi, often seen as the playmaker, seamlessly merged his role with goal-scoring responsibilities, which saw him leading not just in goals but in creative play. Suarez, known for his aggressiveness and ability to capitalize on the slightest of chances, added depth and breadth to the attack. Meanwhile, Neymar's flair and ability to take on defenders added an extra layer of threat on the wings.

The 2015-16 season saw the trio reach its statistical peak in terms of goal contributions, with a combined tally of 131 goals. Their ability to read each other's movements and intentions almost telepathically was a hallmark of their play, making it nearly impossible for defenses to predict or counter their next move.

Together, the trio formed an attacking force that not only mesmerized with its fluidity and intuition but also redefined attacking play in European football.

A Second Treble

Barcelona's second treble, secured in 2015, was a testament to Messi's resilience and leadership after a rocky start to the season. Under the guidance of Luis Enrique, the team had faced internal tensions and early struggles, culminating in a fallout between the coach and Messi in January. However, the squad recovered, propelled by Messi's brilliance, and embarked on a historic run to claim La Liga, the Copa del Rey, and the UEFA Champions League.

Messi had the most complete season of his career, showcasing his versatility and relentless drive. His partnership with Neymar and Suarez in the deadly "MSN" trio was the driving force behind the team's success. Messi contributed decisively throughout the competition, with his dribbling magic and key goals, such as the famous solo effort in the Copa del Rey final against Athletic Bilbao. By the time the Champions League final arrived, Messi was in full stride.

In the 3-1 victory over Juventus, Messi was integral to the team's success. Despite a nervous start, Barcelona quickly took control. In a pivotal moment in the second half, Messi's brilliant dribbling led to Suarez's crucial goal. Messi's ability to deliver in critical moments proved his unwavering commitment to Barcelona's collective success.

The final was the culmination of a season in which Messi, along with Suarez and Neymar, netted an incredible 122 goals in all competitions. Messi's ability to adapt, alongside his attacking prowess, was key in guiding Barcelona to their second treble, cementing his legacy as one of the greatest to ever play the game.

A Record-Breaking Journey

On November 22, 2014, Messi surpassed Telmo Zarra's long-standing record of 251 goals with a stunning hat-trick against Sevilla. This marked his 253rd goal in the Spanish top flight.

Lionel Messi's remarkable achievement of becoming La Liga's all-time top scorer is a testament to his enduring excellence and consistency. Messi's journey to breaking this record was not just about surpassing a number but about consistently raising the bar of footballing excellence. His previous seasons were filled with record-breaking performances, including becoming La Liga's top scorer multiple times, notably in the 2011-12 season with a record 50 goals. Messi also achieved numerous feats, including scoring against every team in La Liga in consecutive matches and registering a staggering number of hat-tricks.

What set Messi apart from others was his ability to remain relentless in his pursuit of greatness, even as defenses tried to adapt to his skill set. His hat-trick against Sevilla was a perfect example of his vision, finishing, and playmaking ability. His first goal was a beautiful chip, the second a clinical finish, and the third was a well-executed strike that showcased his technical brilliance. Messi was more than just a goal scorer—he was the focal point of Barcelona's attacking play, contributing with assists and creating opportunities for his teammates.

Messi's achievement was not only a personal victory but also a reflection of Barcelona's attacking philosophy. His role as the catalyst for their success throughout the years was clear, and as he surpassed Zarra's record, he added yet another chapter to an already illustrious career. In his pursuit of greatness, Messi has become a symbol of what dedication, talent, and consistency can achieve. As Barcelona's all-time top scorer and La Liga's best-ever finisher, Messi's record may stand for years to come.

Coping with Copa América

The 2016 Copa América final between Argentina and Chile ended in heartbreak for Lionel Messi and his team. The match, which ended 0-0 after both regular time and extra time, culminated in a tense penalty shootout that saw Chile emerge victorious 4-2.

The game itself was a scrappy affair, with both teams reduced to 10 men in the first half. Chile's key player was sent off in the 27th minute for a foul on Messi, while an Argentinian member received a red card for a rough challenge 15 minutes later. The match lacked clear-cut chances, with both teams struggling to break through despite moments of individual brilliance. Argentina's goalkeeper was called into action several times, but neither side could find the back of the net during the 90 minutes or the additional 30 minutes of extra time.

The penalty shootout added further agony for Argentina. Messi and other players missed their penalties, while Chile converted the winning penalty, sending the Copa América trophy to Chile for the second consecutive year.

For Messi, the defeat marked his fourth loss in a final with Argentina, a string of near-misses that added to the weight of the disappointment. His missed penalty was particularly painful, as the match had been seen as his chance to claim international glory. Despite his individual success, including becoming Argentina's top scorer, Messi's efforts were ultimately in vain, as Argentina fell short once again.

After Argentina's devastating 4-2 penalty loss to Chile in the 2016 Copa América final, Lionel Messi, who missed Argentina's opening penalty, was visibly crushed. This loss marked his fourth final defeat with the national team, a series of near-misses that seemed to weigh heavily on him. Messi's frustration reached its peak in the aftermath of the match, as he announced his intention to retire from international football.

"I'm done playing with the national team," Messi stated after the match, expressing the deep pain he felt. "I tried my hardest. It's been four finals, and I was not able to win. It hurts me more than anyone, but it is evident that this is not for me." Despite being Argentina's all-time leading scorer with 55 goals in 113 appearances, Messi had been unable to lead his country to a major international title, losing in the 2014 World Cup final and the 2015 Copa América final against Chile.

Although other players also expressed their disappointment and hinted at retirement, the goalkeeper remained hopeful that Messi's decision was made in the heat of the moment, stating, "I can't imagine the national team without Messi."

Messi's potential retirement sparked a wave of emotion among Argentina fans, as his greatness for Barcelona was unquestioned, but his national team career had yet to match that level of success.

But this retirement from international football was brief. Lionel Messi soon announced his return to the national team. The Barcelona star revealed through his management that his passion for Argentina was too strong to walk away for good. "I gave serious thought to quitting, but my love for my country and this shirt is too great," Messi said in a statement.

Argentina's new coach, Edgardo Bauza, confirmed Messi's return, expressing confidence in his star forward's eagerness to rejoin the squad.

CHAPTER 14
RECORDS, RED CARDS, AND REDEMPTION

Legends Rise

The clock was ticking down, the tension rising. With each passing second, it seemed like Barcelona's hopes of clinching a dramatic victory at the Bernabéu were slipping away.

But then, in the dying moments of injury time, Lionel Messi arrived at the perfect moment.

The match had been a rollercoaster of emotions. Real Madrid initially took the lead in the 28th minute with a close-range goal. However, Barcelona quickly responded five minutes later when Messi produced a brilliant solo run and finish to equalize. In the second half, Barcelona regained the lead in the 73rd minute thanks to Ivan Rakitic's stunning long-range strike. But Real Madrid wasn't done, and despite being reduced to 10 men after a red card, they equalized in the 85th.

Just when it seemed like the match would end in a draw, Messi delivered.

A defender's run from deep in the team's half found a left-back, whose cross to the forward was met with clinical precision, sending the ball into the net and sealing the victory. It was a fitting moment for Messi, who had been instrumental in both Barcelona's attack and defense throughout the game, despite taking a blow to the face from Marcelo earlier. His 500th goal was not just a milestone but a statement—one that would secure his place as the all-time great in Barcelona's storied history.

In a do-or-die World Cup qualifier against Ecuador, Lionel Messi once again proved why he's regarded as one of the greatest players of all time. Argentina, struggling in the qualification campaign, found themselves behind within the first minute after Ecuador's player fired in a stunning goal. With Argentina's World Cup hopes hanging by a thread, Messi took charge.

Just 12 minutes later, Messi equalized with a calm finish from an Angel Di Maria cross. But he wasn't done. Nine minutes after that, Messi showcased his brilliance once more, sidestepping a feeble challenge to drive the ball past Ecuador's keeper at the near post. The game was far from over, but Messi, with his back to the wall, scored his third and final goal in a moment of magic. Collecting a loose ball, he darted towards the goal and chipped it delicately over the goalkeeper, securing Argentina's spot in the 2018 World Cup.

Messi's hat-trick single-handedly transformed a tense, high-pressure situation into a triumphant one, ensuring Argentina's place in Russia and cementing his role as the hero when it mattered most.

Seeing Red

The fiery third-place match between Argentina and Chile at the 2019 Copa America did not go the way anyone imagined. Lionel Messi received his first red card in 14 years. After Argentina's 2-1 win over Chile in the third-place match of the 2019 Copa America, Lionel Messi was left fuming, not celebrating. The Barcelona star had been sent off in the first half for a contentious shoulder-barging clash with Chile's Gary Medel, with both players shown red cards.

The decision was controversial, with many feeling it warranted only yellow cards, especially given the lack of serious aggression. The referee's decision stood despite VAR's review, leaving Messi visibly aggrieved. This moment encapsulated the frustration Messi felt, not just from the match, but from a string of near misses in finals with Argentina.

As he walked off the field, Argentina had already sealed a 2-1 win, but Messi's fiery reaction to the decision highlighted the pain of never winning a major title with his country. Messi was visibly frustrated with the decision and refused to participate in the medal ceremony that followed.

After Argentina's loss to Brazil in the 2019 Copa America, Lionel Messi addressed his teammates with heartfelt words that moved everyone to tears. "I'm proud of the team we've built," Messi told them. "We may not have been together for long, but it feels like we've known each other for years. We've all worked together from day one, and I'm proud of the youngsters for their dedication. They earned their place here." His speech, especially to the younger players, was emotional, urging them to continue working hard. Di Maria noted, "It touched everyone's hearts, especially the young players. They have to carry on the path, and eventually, luck will be on our side."

However, it was his explosive post-match comments that truly drew attention. Messi accused the tournament organizers of corruption, stating, "There is no doubt, the whole thing is set up for Brazil." He believed that his comments against Brazil in the semifinal had led to his punishment. Messi had criticized the refereeing in the semifinal, where Argentina lost 2-0 to Brazil, accusing the officials of being biased and not reviewing penalty incidents through VAR. He claimed that the competition was designed for Brazil to win, saying, "I didn't want to be part of this corruption, we shouldn't have to be part of this disrespect."

The frustration of losing out in back-to-back finals, along with his suspicions about the competition's fairness, led Messi to speak candidly about the shortcomings of the Copa America. He concluded by saying, "I always tell the truth and I'm honest, that is what keeps me calm, if what I say has repercussions that is not my business."

Lionel Messi's Copa America experience was a rollercoaster, ending with an unexpected red card against Chile and controversial remarks accusing CONMEBOL of corruption.

Although some Barcelona fans wished Messi would retire from international duty to preserve his prime years, Messi's connection with Argentina had never been stronger. His passion for the national team was evident as he passionately sang the anthem and defended his teammates after tough losses. Messi's renewed commitment to the national team, along with a fresh, hungry squad, could have reignited his focus and intensity, ultimately benefiting his Barcelona form. If Messi had been able to channel this determination, the already world-class player might have led Argentina to success in the 2020 Copa América, with the motivation of winning it at home.

A Historic Triumph

Lionel Messi cemented his place in football history by winning his sixth Ballon d'Or on December 2, 2019, at the Théâtre du Châtelet in Paris. The award, given to the world's best player, placed him one ahead of his long-time rival Cristiano Ronaldo, making him the most decorated player in the award's history. The Barcelona and Argentina forward edged out Virgil van Dijk, who had played a crucial role in Liverpool's Champions League victory, as well as Ronaldo and Sadio Mané in the final voting.

Messi's 2018-19 season was nothing short of extraordinary. He led

Barcelona to their 10th La Liga title in his career and finished as the top scorer in Spain and Europe. His 36 goals in La Liga secured him his sixth European Golden Shoe, while his 12 goals in the Champions League made him the competition's leading scorer. In total, he scored 51 goals in 50 matches across all competitions, surpassing the 600-goal mark for Barcelona. However, the season also had its disappointments, with Barcelona's shocking 4-0 UCL semifinal defeat to Liverpool and Argentina's Copa América heartbreak.

In his acceptance speech, Messi reflected on his journey since his first Ballon d'Or win in 2009, recalling that he had been 22 years old at the time. "A few years ago, I received my first Ballon d'Or here in Paris. It was something unthinkable. Today is my sixth. As my wife always tells me, never stop dreaming," he said. The Argentine acknowledged that time was passing quickly but hoped to continue competing at the highest level for a few more years.

Messi's return to the top came a year after Luka Modrić broke his and Ronaldo's decade-long dominance of the Ballon d'Or. With this victory, Messi reaffirmed his position as the greatest player of his generation.

CHAPTER 15
THE NIGHT BARCELONA FELL

A Historic Humiliation

On August 14, 2020, Bayern Munich delivered one of the most brutal defeats in Champions League history, demolishing Barcelona 8-2 in a one-sided quarterfinal in Lisbon. This result not only marked Barcelona's worst-ever European defeat but also underscored the glaring differences between the two sides. Bayern's relentless high-pressing, energy, and efficiency overwhelmed a Barcelona team that looked disjointed and unprepared.

The match started at a blistering pace, with the opposition taking the lead in just the fourth minute through a forward, who combined brilliantly with another striker. Barcelona briefly responded when a defender scored an own goal, but from that moment onward, the Spanish giants were torn apart. Two wingers and the forward all found the net before halftime, leaving the team 4-1 down and in complete disarray.

A forward gave Barcelona a glimmer of hope early in the second half, but that was quickly extinguished by a young full-back's sensational solo run, which set up a midfielder for the opposition's fifth. Things went from bad to worse for Barcelona when a player, on loan from the club to the opposition, came off the bench to score twice and assist the striker's 14th goal of the tournament. By the final whistle, Barcelona were left humiliated, suffering their worst European defeat since losing 8-0 to a team in 1946.

This victory was a warning to the rest of Europe. Bayern had already won the Bundesliga and the German Cup and now looked unstoppable in their pursuit of a sixth Champions League title. Their high-intensity, attacking style under Hansi Flick was proving deadly, with 39 goals scored in the competition and only eight conceded.

Their next challenge would be against Lyon in the semifinal, while Paris Saint-Germain and RB Leipzig were set to clash in the other semifinal, in a tournament format being played behind closed doors due to the COVID-19 pandemic. With no fans in Lisbon, Bayern's dominance on the pitch spoke louder than any roaring crowd.

For Barcelona, this was not just a loss; it was a defining moment of decline. Gerard Piqué admitted, "We have hit rock bottom," as calls for major changes grew louder. Quique Setién, the under-pressure manager, was expected to be dismissed, while veterans like Sergio Busquets, Jordi Alba, and even Luis Suárez faced uncertain futures.

This 8-2 humiliation was more than just a game—it was the night an era at Barcelona truly ended. It was also the first time since 2008 that Barcelona finished a season without a major trophy, an unthinkable situation for a club of their stature. Public disputes between players and club officials throughout the season had already exposed internal instability, but this defeat made it undeniable—Barcelona were no longer among Europe's elite.

Bayern, meanwhile, showed no mercy and no weakness. The five-time European champions were on a mission to reclaim their place at the top, and after such an emphatic victory, few doubted that they would go all the way.

Most notably, Lionel Messi was visibly devastated. For years, he had carried Barcelona almost single-handedly, but this defeat highlighted how desperately the club needed a rebuild.

A Shocking Declaration

On August 25, 2020, Lionel Messi officially informed Barcelona that he wanted to leave the club, marking a dramatic turning point in one of football's greatest careers. After spending nearly two decades at Barcelona, winning 34 trophies, and setting countless records, the Argentine legend had finally reached his breaking point. His decision came just 11 days after Barcelona's humiliating 8-2 defeat to Bayern Munich in the Champions League, a loss that capped a trophy-less season and deepened the club's crisis.

Messi explained that his decision to leave was not a sudden reaction to Barcelona's humiliating 8-2 Champions League loss to Bayern Munich, but the result of a long-standing disagreement with the club's leadership and its lack of a clear sporting project.

Messi claimed that he had been expressing his desire to leave for over a year, regularly telling the club manager that he believed his time at Barcelona was over. The Argentine cited the club's failure to bring in young, competitive players and poor planning as reasons for his unhappiness. He also accused the club of breaking their word, stating that he had been repeatedly assured he could leave for free at the end of the season, only for the club to later insist that the deadline for activating the clause had passed.

In a dramatic turn, Messi sent a burofax to Barcelona to formally request his departure, making his stance legally official. While some club figures criticized this move as unnecessary, Messi defended it, stating that if he hadn't taken that step, Barcelona would have ignored his request. He described the past year as one of the most difficult of his career, admitting that he suffered during training and matches, struggling to find motivation in a club that had lost direction.

Barcelona confirmed Messi's request but hinted that a legal battle could follow. The dispute centered around a contract clause allowing Messi to leave for free at the end of the season. The club insisted the deadline had expired in June, but Messi's camp argued that the extended season due to COVID-19 meant the clause was still valid. If forced to buy out his contract, any club wanting Messi would need to pay his staggering €700 million ($826 million) release clause—a sum few could afford.

Messi's likely destinations included Manchester City, where he could reunite with Pep Guardiola, or Paris Saint-Germain, home to Neymar and Kylian Mbappé. Former Barcelona star Gary Lineker expressed hope that the club would respect Messi's loyalty and not obstruct his departure. Meanwhile, club legend Carles Puyol publicly supported Messi, tweeting, "Respect and admiration, Leo. You have all my support."

The turmoil at Barcelona had been building throughout the season. Messi had publicly clashed with club officials, particularly the sporting director Éric Abidal, who was fired days before Messi's announcement. The newly appointed coach had already begun reshaping the squad, reportedly telling other veterans they were no longer in his plans.

Messi ultimately chose to stay to avoid a legal battle with the club he loved. He emphasized that his commitment to Barcelona remained strong, but his faith in its leadership had been broken. The saga ended with Bartomeu under immense pressure, with many fans and club officials seeing Messi's dissatisfaction as further evidence of the board's failure.

This incident not only marked a low point in Messi's relationship with Barcelona but also signaled the beginning of the end of his legendary tenure at the club. Less than a year later, Messi would depart for Paris

Saint-Germain, closing a historic chapter in Barcelona's golden era.

Shining in the Finals

On April 17, 2021, Lionel Messi led Barcelona to a dominant 4-0 victory over Athletic Bilbao in the Copa del Rey final, delivering a masterclass performance that left fans wondering—was this a new beginning or a farewell gift?

Scoring twice and dictating the game's tempo, Messi once again proved why he remained one of football's greatest.

The match at La Cartuja Stadium in Seville saw Barcelona clinch their 31st Copa del Rey title, ending a two-year trophy drought. The final was Messi at his finest—dribbling through defenders, orchestrating attacks, and scoring two stunning goals. His performance, alongside key contributions from Antoine Griezmann, Frenkie de Jong, and Jordi Alba, dismantled Bilbao in a devastating 12-minute second-half blitz.

While most top strikers were celebrated for reaching 15-20 goals per season, Messi made 30+ goals a routine achievement for over a decade. His dazzling footwork, precise finishing, and ability to dictate the game's tempo showcased why he was beyond comparison. In a night where Barcelona reclaimed silverware, Messi was the heart of it all, delivering yet another masterclass performance that further solidified his GOAT status.

Yet, Messi's beaming smile as he lifted the trophy sparked more speculation than celebration. Was he savoring another triumph with Barcelona, or was he cherishing what might be his last title with the club? The Argentine avoided discussing his future post-match, instead acknowledging the unusual circumstances of celebrating without fans.

The uncertainty surrounding Messi's future had loomed over Barcelona all season. He maintained that he would decide his future when his contract expired in June 2021.

The club however, remained optimistic. "Leo is the best player in the world, and he has deep roots here. I believe he wants to stay, and we will do everything to keep him," he said. Meanwhile, his coach admitted he was hoping for the best, stating, "We hope this is not Messi's last Copa. We want him to stay with us."

Barcelona's Copa del Rey triumph came at a pivotal moment. The club's financial troubles had left them struggling in the transfer market, and the departure of key players had hurt their attack. The team had also failed to win La Liga in 2020 and suffered their worst-ever Champions League defeat to Bayern Munich.

For Messi, this victory was another reminder of his enduring brilliance, even at age 33. His two goals took his Barcelona career tally to 35 major titles, further cementing his legacy. But the biggest question remained—would this be Messi's final triumph in a Barcelona shirt?

As speculation mounted, one thing was certain: Messi had once again delivered when it mattered most, proving that regardless of his future, his impact on Barcelona would be unforgettable.

Why Lionel Messi Left Barcelona (Again)

Barcelona's statement was brief, cold, and almost surreal: "Leo Messi will not continue at FC Barcelona due to La Liga's financial regulations."

The announcement sent shockwaves through the football world. Even though Barcelona's financial struggles had been widely reported, no one truly believed that Messi—the club's greatest-ever player—would actually leave. The confusion, disbelief, and eventual heartbreak unfolded over the next few days as fans, players, and even Messi himself struggled to come to terms with the unthinkable.

At first, many refused to believe it. It lacked the emotional farewell that a player of Messi's stature deserved, leading many to wonder if it was a bluff—a last-minute negotiation tactic to pressure La Liga into making an exception. The silence from Messi and his teammates in the immediate aftermath only deepened the sense of uncertainty. Fans held on to hope, believing that Barcelona would find a way, just as they had in the past.

Then, Joan Laporta spoke. The club president explained that despite Messi's willingness to stay, Barcelona simply could not register his contract under La Liga's salary cap rules. Even if Messi had accepted a 50% pay cut, the club's debt was so severe that his wages remained unaffordable. Laporta's words confirmed the worst fears, but many were still in denial. Some questioned whether every possible solution had been explored, and rumors began circulating about last-minute efforts to change the situation. Could Messi play for free? Would La Liga intervene? Could another financial 'lever' be pulled?

When Messi finally spoke, the reality set in. He admitted that he had been blindsided by the situation, believing everything had been arranged for his renewal. In an emotional press conference on August 8, he confirmed that his time at Barcelona was over.

"I thought it was all sorted… but this time, it's not coming back."

There were tears, not just from Messi, but from fans who had grown up watching him define an era. His farewell speech made it clear: this was not how he wanted to leave.

The streets of Barcelona were filled with devastated fans, many wearing his jersey, chanting his name in protest. There were banners outside Camp Nou, some blaming Laporta, others pointing at the La Liga president. At the same time, there was an eerie silence—it was as if Barcelona, the club, the city, and its people, had lost part of their identity overnight.

Among his former teammates, the reactions were mixed. Players like Gerard Piqué, Sergio Busquets, and Jordi Alba all posted tributes, expressing shock and sadness. Some players, however, remained unusually quiet, possibly reflecting their own frustrations with how the situation had been handled. Meanwhile, across the football world, figures like Neymar, Luis Suárez, and even Cristiano Ronaldo acknowledged the end of an era.

Though the mourning was intense, the world moved on quickly. Barcelona reassigned Messi's iconic No.10 shirt to another player, and despite some protests, fans returned to Camp Nou as the season started. But the scars remained. For many, Messi's departure wasn't just about losing a player—it was the symbolic end of Barcelona's golden age, an admission that the club had fallen from its once-dominant position.

Lionel Messi's dream of returning to Barcelona in 2023 ultimately collapsed due to the same reason he had to leave in 2021—the club's financial instability and La Liga's strict salary cap rules. Despite Messi's preference to rejoin Barcelona, the club was simply not in a position to register him without significant player sales and salary reductions, which could not be completed in time.

Barcelona's struggles stemmed from La Liga's salary cap rules, which restrict clubs from spending beyond a certain percentage of their revenue. Even though Joan Laporta and the Barcelona board were desperate to bring Messi back, they could not offer him any written guarantees that he would be registered. The club needed to offload players and reduce wages before they could sign Messi, but no major sales had been completed at the time of his decision.

La Liga had recently approved Barcelona's viability plan for the upcoming season, allowing them to register contracts for other players, but it was still not enough to accommodate Messi's salary. Messi had verbally agreed to a €25 million-a-year contract, meaning Barcelona needed to free up approximately €70 million in salaries to sign him. This would have required rushed player sales, which were unlikely to happen before preseason training began on July 10.

The head coach had not yet spoken to players about potential departures, making it impossible for Barcelona to generate the financial flexibility needed within the timeline Messi required. Many players were rumored to be on the market, but none of them had been sold when Messi made his decision.

Beyond the logistical issues, Messi was also uncomfortable with the financial sacrifices Barcelona employees would have to make to accommodate his return. The club was already executing cost-cutting measures, including a 15% reduction across various sports divisions, and even shutting down its in-house channel, Barça TV—a network that had documented Messi's career from the start.

Messi was concerned about being perceived as the reason for staff layoffs and budget reductions, stating:

"I heard Barcelona had to sell players or make pay cuts, and the truth is I didn't want to go through that or feel responsible."

It was over. For real.

CHAPTER 16
A NEW CHAPTER IN PARIS

Messi's Transfer to PSG

Lionel Messi, the football legend with six Ballon d'Or awards under his belt, arrived in Paris on a warm Tuesday afternoon. His journey from Barcelona, where he had spent 21 years, culminated in a medical examination and the signing of a two-year contract with Paris Saint-Germain, with an option for a third year. The contract, reportedly worth £25 million per year after tax, plus bonuses, also included a £25 million signing-on fee. Messi would don the No 30 shirt, a number that held sentimental value as it was the one he wore during his debut for Barcelona back in 2003.

Upon his arrival in Paris, Messi expressed his enthusiasm for this new chapter. "I am excited to begin a new chapter of my career at Paris Saint-Germain," he declared. "Everything about the club matches my football ambitions. I know how talented the squad and the coaching staff are here. I am determined to help build something special for the club and the fans, and I am looking forward to stepping out onto the pitch at the Parc des Princes."

PSG's chairman, Nasser Al-Khelaifi, was equally thrilled. "I am delighted that Lionel Messi has chosen to join Paris Saint-Germain and we are proud to welcome him and his family to Paris," he said. "He has made no secret of his desire to continue competing at the very highest level and winning trophies, and naturally our ambition as a club is to do the same."

The decision to join PSG was influenced by several factors, including the club's potential to compete for major trophies like the Champions League. Additionally, there was the allure of reuniting with Neymar, his former teammate from Barcelona with whom he had shared numerous victories.

Messi's first press conference as a PSG player was scheduled for the following Wednesday morning at the Parc des Princes. The football world watched eagerly, not just for Messi's words but for the new era he was about to usher in at PSG. His transfer was not just a change of clubs; it was a seismic shift in the landscape of European football, bringing new hopes and dreams to the fans in Paris while leaving a void in the heart of Barcelona.

Parisian Debut

Lionel Messi, at 34, embarked on a new journey as he made his debut for Paris Saint-Germain (PSG) in a Ligue 1 match against Reims, which concluded in a 2-0 victory. The game was broadcast on Spain's free-to-air channel Telecinco, drawing an unprecedented 2.2 million average viewers, making it the most-watched French football match in Spanish television history. Over 6.7 million viewers tuned in at some point, highlighting the immense interest in Messi's first game outside Barcelona.

The match itself was a significant event, not just for the viewership but for the footballing world watching Messi step onto the pitch in the 66th minute, replacing Neymar. Wearing his new No 30 shirt, Messi received a standing ovation from a full house at Stade Auguste-Delaune. The Argentine, whose career until then had been exclusively with Barcelona, was warmly welcomed by fans chanting his name, despite only being named on the bench initially.

During his 24-minute cameo, Messi showed flashes of his brilliance. He played several nice passes and was part of some effective link-up plays, although his opportunities in the penalty area were limited. The atmosphere was electric, with ticket prices having soared to around 6,000 euros, a stark contrast to the initial sales of only about 6,000 before his signing was announced.

Kylian Mbappe scored both goals for PSG, overshadowing Messi's debut.

His performance included a header from an Angel di Maria cross for the first goal and a sweeping finish from a right-back's delivery for the second.

Yet, the focus remained on Messi, whose every touch was met with anticipation.

Post-match, PSG coach Mauricio Pochettino spoke highly of Messi's influence, even in such a brief appearance. "He brought serenity to the team. His energy and his optimism trickled down on the rest of the team," Pochettino noted, emphasizing Messi's impact beyond just the scoreboard. He also mentioned that Messi was still far from his best form but was optimistic about his integration into the team.

This debut was not just a game; it was a cultural moment. While Messi did not score or have a direct goal involvement, his presence was felt, both on the field and in the hearts of football fans around the globe. The match also highlighted the contrast between Messi's new chapter with PSG and his former club, Barcelona, whose game against Getafe on the same day drew significantly fewer viewers.

Additionally, the game was streamed on Twitch, attracting another massive audience, underlining Messi's draw across different platforms. The rights to Ligue 1 in Spain had been secured by Gerard Pique's company, which planned to sublicense them, showcasing the strategic moves made in anticipation of Messi's impact.

As Messi adapted to his new environment in Paris, his debut was a testament to his enduring appeal and the excitement he brought to football, even in a new league and country.

Seventh

Lionel Messi did it again.

The Argentine maestro added his seventh Ballon d'Or to his collection on November 29, 2021, further solidifying his status as one of the greatest football players of all time. This latest accolade put Messi two Ballon d'Ors ahead of his long-time rival, Cristiano Ronaldo. His journey to this prestigious title was filled with triumphs, challenges, and resilience in a season that tested him like never before.

Messi's path to the 2021 Ballon d'Or was marked by both highs and lows. After a turbulent departure from Barcelona, where financial constraints forced him to leave the club he had called home for over 20 years, he found a new challenge at Paris Saint-Germain (PSG). Despite struggling with injuries and adapting to a new league, Messi's brilliance remained undeniable. His first major international trophy with Argentina, the 2021 Copa América, became a career-defining moment. He led Argentina to their first major title in 28 years, winning both the Golden Boot and Player of the Tournament awards.

In club football, Messi's final season at Barcelona had been bittersweet. He helped the club win the Copa del Rey, scoring twice in the final, but Barcelona fell short in La Liga, failing to win the title. Despite the club's struggles, Messi finished as La Liga's top scorer with 30 goals, earning his eighth Pichichi Trophy. His consistency in front of goal ensured that even in a difficult season, he remained the standout performer for Barcelona.

While many believed Robert Lewandowski had a strong case for the Ballon d'Or due to his record-breaking season with Bayern Munich, Messi's achievements in 2021 were impossible to ignore. He netted 41 goals and provided 17 assists, proving his excellence despite his team's challenges. His Copa América victory, coupled with his dominance in La Liga, ultimately secured him the award.

During his acceptance speech, Messi acknowledged Lewandowski's remarkable achievements and stated that the Polish striker deserved the 2020 Ballon d'Or, which had been controversially canceled due to the COVID-19 pandemic. His words reflected sportsmanship and humility, adding to the integrity of his own victory.

The 2021 Ballon d'Or marked another milestone in Messi's illustrious career. At 34 years old, his hunger for success remained undiminished. As he embarked on the next chapter with PSG, the football world wondered: How many more Ballon d'Ors would Messi claim before retiring? Only time would tell, but with his talent, work ethic, and determination, there was every possibility that he would add even more to his legendary collection.

Historic Wins

Lionel Messi continued to break records as Paris Saint-Germain secured an 11th Ligue 1 title with a 1-1 draw at Strasbourg, cementing their place in history. Messi's goal, a brilliant finish following a perfect pass from Kylian Mbappé, marked his 496th in Europe's top five leagues, surpassing Cristiano Ronaldo's previous record of 495 goals. This goal was his 32nd for PSG, a milestone that could potentially be his last, with his departure expected this summer.

Despite being on the brink of securing the title, PSG faced jeers from their own supporters. As the first half came to a close, a chorus of boos echoed through the stadium, reflecting the fans' frustration with the team's mediocre performance in the opening 45 minutes. Neymar and Messi were particularly targeted with criticism from the stands following that defeat.

This title also saw PSG surpass the records of Saint-Étienne and Marseille, both of whom had won 10 French titles. Messi's goal in the title-deciding match ensured his time at PSG would end on a more positive note than anticipated after a turbulent start to May, which included a two-week suspension for an unauthorized trip to Saudi Arabia.

Soon after, in one of the most dramatic World Cup finals in history, Lionel Messi and Argentina triumphed over France in a penalty shootout to claim their third World Cup title. After a 3-3 draw that stretched through extra time, Argentina defeated France 4-2 on penalties, with Messi playing a pivotal role throughout the match. It was Messi's last World Cup and the culmination of a lifelong pursuit, finally securing his place among footballing immortals with a victory in the tournament that had eluded him for so long.

The match was a fierce spectacle, with Argentina taking an early 2-0 lead. Messi opened the scoring in the 23rd minute with a calm penalty after an Argentine midfielder was fouled by a French forward. The first half was dominated by Argentina, who quickly doubled their lead thanks to a brilliant counter-attack orchestrated by Messi.

He found an Argentine midfielder, who squared the ball to another midfielder for a composed finish.

However, the second half saw a remarkable turnaround by France. Mbappé, who had been largely quiet up until that point, turned the game on its head. A penalty in the 80th minute brought France back into the game, and just minutes later, Mbappé scored another stunning goal to level the score at 2-2, sending the match into extra time.

Extra time was equally dramatic. Messi scored again, putting Argentina ahead, only for Mbappé to net his third goal, completing an extraordinary World Cup final hat-trick, and forcing the game to be decided by penalties.

In the shootout, after an early goal from Mbappé, Argentina took control. Messi calmly converted his penalty, and Emiliano Martínez saved Kingsley Coman's attempt, giving Argentina a lead they would not relinquish. With the shootout tied 2-2, Gonzalo Montiel slotted home the winning penalty, securing Argentina's victory.

The win ended Argentina's 36-year wait for a World Cup title, a feat that seemed impossible just a few years ago. Messi, who finished the tournament with seven goals, was once again the heart of the team, proving that age and adversity could not diminish his brilliance. With this victory, Messi silenced critics and completed his illustrious career with the ultimate achievement: a World Cup win. The victory not only marked a personal triumph for Messi but also cemented Argentina's place in World Cup history.

CHAPTER 17
A NEW BEGINNING

The Final Chapter

Speculation was starting to grow over Messi's future. His contract was set to expire in the summer of 2023. The speculation intensified after PSG's early exit from the Champions League, coupled with Messi's strained relationship with fans, as shown by the boos during key matches.

The news eventually became clear: Lionel Messi did not remain a Paris Saint-Germain player beyond the 2022-23 season. After months of speculation, his time in Paris officially came to an end. Messi's contract expired in June 2023, and despite initial plans for an extension, a series of events caused significant cracks in the relationship between the club and its superstar. His departure became inevitable, and his team soon began searching for his next destination.

The tipping point came after a controversial incident where Messi was suspended for two weeks for missing a training session without prior approval. As part of his role as a tourism ambassador for Saudi Arabia, Messi traveled despite PSG's strict directive to remain in Paris. This was perceived as a challenge to the club's authority, leading PSG—historically lenient with its star players—to take an unprecedented step by suspending him. It was the first such punishment under Qatari ownership since 2011.

However, the rift between Messi and PSG ran deeper.

Although the two sides initially agreed in principle to extend his contract before the 2022 World Cup, the relationship soured in the following months. Messi's performances in key Champions League matches—particularly against Bayern Munich—led to doubts within the club. PSG's ultimate goal was to win the Champions League, and Messi's failure to make a decisive impact in crucial knockout games cast doubt on his importance to their long-term plans.

As PSG struggled to convince Messi to stay, his camp explored other options. His former club, Barcelona, hoped for a reunion, but financial restrictions made a return difficult. Meanwhile, Al Hilal from Saudi

Arabia made a serious offer, creating the possibility of Messi following Cristiano Ronaldo to the Middle East. Further hinting at his exit, Messi's children were not re-enrolled in a Parisian school for the next academic year, signaling that a move away from France was imminent.

Messi's departure from PSG marked the end of a turbulent chapter. His time in Paris wasn't the fairytale many expected, but it remained another part of his extraordinary football legacy.

Lionel Messi's time at Paris Saint-Germain left him with mixed feelings, especially after winning the 2022 World Cup with Argentina. Messi found it difficult to adjust to life in Paris and revealed that he felt a "fracture with a significant group of PSG fans." Despite his unparalleled achievement on the world stage, Messi resented not being recognized by PSG for his World Cup success. While all his Argentina teammates were celebrated by their respective clubs, Messi was the only player out of 25 not to receive any club recognition upon his return to Paris.

Looking back, Messi admitted that his time at PSG wasn't as he had expected. However, he acknowledged that "things happen for a reason," and even though he wasn't entirely happy, winning the World Cup while at PSG was a significant and rewarding chapter in his career.

Move to Inter Miami

Lionel Messi's highly anticipated move to Inter Miami CF was officially confirmed, marking the beginning of an exciting new chapter in his illustrious career. The 36-year-old Argentine superstar signed a contract with the Major League Soccer (MLS) club that ran through the end of the 2025 season. Messi's arrival, after his departure from Paris Saint-Germain, signaled a new era for both the player and MLS.

Messi, who earned between £50 million and $60 million per year, expressed his excitement about joining Inter Miami, saying, "I'm very excited to start this next step in my career with Inter Miami and in the United States." He also emphasized the importance of working together with the club to achieve their goals. Messi was first available for selection in a July 21 Leagues Cup match against Cruz Azul.

This move followed Messi's decision to reject a return to Barcelona and a lucrative offer from Saudi Arabia. It marked a significant moment in MLS history, as Messi was expected to help raise the league's profile globally. He was reunited with former Barcelona teammates Sergio

Busquets and Jordi Alba, as well as former coach Gerardo "Tata" Martino.

Messi's arrival in Miami came at a time when the club was struggling in the MLS standings, but his presence was expected to boost the team's performance and bring attention to the sport in the United States.

Lionel Messi's decision to leave Paris Saint-Germain and embark on a new journey in Major League Soccer marked the next phase of his illustrious career. Despite receiving offers from Barcelona and the Middle East, Messi chose to pursue the American dream with Inter Miami in the summer of 2023.

Messi was also particularly drawn to the appeal of Miami as a vibrant, bilingual city with strong ties to Latin American culture, making it an ideal place for his family. The footballing aspect of the move also influenced his decision, as Messi saw it as an opportunity to make a lasting impact on American soccer.

After leaving PSG in June, Messi reflected on the positive shift in his life since joining Inter Miami CF. He spoke about how he now enjoys football in a new way, relishing his time with the club. He emphasized that retirement was not on his mind, as he still enjoyed playing the game. Messi shared his decision to move to Miami was driven by the different experience and the joy it brought him.

Messi also entertained the idea of returning to his boyhood club, Newell's Old Boys, before he retires, especially after achieving the pinnacle of football success with Argentina. He was uncertain about the future, including his participation in the 2026 World Cup, but confirmed he would play in the 2024 Copa América, focusing on his day-to-day performances rather than dwelling on what lies ahead.

Lionel Messi's arrival at Inter Miami had been nothing short of transformative for the club, both on and off the field, significantly enhancing its economic standing and global profile. Since signing with Inter Miami in July 2023 on a contract valued at approximately $150 million, the club's financial landscape had undergone a dramatic shift.

Firstly, the economic impact on Inter Miami had been profound. According to reports from ESPN, the club's revenue had almost doubled from an estimated $50-$60 million in 2022 to $120-$130 million in 2023. By 2024, projections suggested that Inter Miami would have surpassed $200 million in revenue, setting a new club record. This financial surge was largely attributed to Messi's global appeal, which had led to a spike in sponsorship deals, ticket sales, and merchandise, particularly jerseys.

The sponsorship sector had seen a remarkable boom. Inter Miami's status as an international brand had attracted partnerships with major corporations like Audi, JPMorgan Chase, Duracell, Lowe's, Visa, and LaCroix. Notably, deals with Fracht and Royal Caribbean for jersey sponsorships had set new records for Major League Soccer (MLS), highlighting the club's elevated marketability. The international allure brought by Messi had enabled Inter Miami to forge partnerships that extended far beyond local or national interest, positioning the club as a global entity.

Jersey sales had been a clear indicator of Messi's impact. His Inter Miami CF jersey was the best-selling sports jersey in the Adidas sports portfolio in 2023 and 2024, and it led the MLS rankings in both years, despite him signing midseason in 2023. The jerseys of his teammates, Luis Suárez, Sergio Busquets, and Jordi Alba, also saw significant sales, indicating the overall boost in interest in the team.

The demand for tickets had been unprecedented. Messi's debut match against Cruz Azul had attracted thousands to Chase Stadium, with fans lining up around the block to purchase the now-iconic 2023 pink home kit. Season tickets for 2024 had sold out months before the schedule was even released, with renewals at a club record 90%, one of the highest rates in the league. Inter Miami's tickets were among the most expensive in MLS, reflecting the premium fans were willing to pay for the Messi experience.

Beyond match days, Messi's influence had extended to merchandise sales. The team store at Chase Stadium had seen continuous crowds, leading to the decision to open it year-round rather than just on game days. The club had capitalized on Messi's global fame during the off-season, participating in a global tour playing matches in El Salvador, Saudi Arabia, Hong Kong, and Japan, further showcasing the economic benefits of his presence.

The long-term vision for Inter Miami had also been influenced by Messi's arrival. The club had begun construction on Miami Freedom Park, a new stadium project with extensive community benefits, hoping that Messi would inaugurate the new venue. His contract, running through the 2025 MLS season with an option for 2026, had given the club leverage in promoting season ticket sales and attracting potential sponsors for the future.

Sealing Victory

Lionel Messi's debut with Inter Miami in the Leagues Cup was set to take place against Liga MX side Cruz Azul, a team that endured a rocky start to the 2023 Apertura season. With a 0-0-3 record, Cruz Azul failed to impress, struggling both defensively and offensively. Despite their historical success, including a dominant run in the '70s that earned them seven championships, the team had developed a reputation for dramatic failures in crucial moments. This "Cruzazulear" phenomenon, where the club repeatedly faltered in big matches, had become a fixture in Mexican soccer culture.

Cruz Azul's struggles were compounded by internal turmoil, with the coach and the club's front office at odds about the team's direction. Defensive lapses and a lack of creativity on the field left them vulnerable. With only one goal in over 270 minutes of play this season, the team seemed in disarray, relying on individual moments of brilliance rather than cohesive team effort. Facing Messi and Inter Miami, Cruz Azul would need to step up dramatically if they were to pull off a surprising victory.

In his Major League Soccer debut, Lionel Messi delivered an unforgettable performance, scoring a brilliant free kick in the 94th minute to give Inter Miami a dramatic 2-1 win over Cruz Azul. The match, part of the Leagues Cup, saw Messi entering in the second half, with the game tied at 1-1 after A Mexican forward's equalizer for Cruz Azul. Prior to Messi's entrance, Robert Taylor had given Miami the lead with a goal just before halftime.

As the game entered its final moments, Messi stepped up to take the free kick, bending it past the Cruz Azul goalkeeper into the top corner, sealing the win for his new team. The fans erupted in cheers as Messi showed his magic on the pitch, marking a perfect debut and an early indication of his impact on MLS.

And Messi continued to set the field ablaze.

In the FIFA Club World Cup, Lionel Messi stepped onto the pitch with an urgency that only a champion could understand. It was his moment to prove, once again, why he was the player the world couldn't stop talking about. After coming off the bench in the 58th minute, Messi ignited the game, as if he was always meant to play in that very moment.

Trailing 2-0, Inter Miami needed something special, and Messi was there to deliver. Suarez had already scored twice, helping to pull Miami back into the game, but it was Messi who took the reins in the final stretch. Within 11 minutes, he scored a hat-trick that sent the stadium into a frenzy, sealing the game 6-2 and breaking the MLS regular season points record.

He found the net first with a blistering strike into the bottom corner, then linked up beautifully with Jordi Alba, before finishing off the game with a perfect volleyed cross from his former Barcelona teammate. It was magic—pure Messi magic. In just minutes, he had turned the tide and made it clear that the Argentinian was back to his best after a two-month injury absence.

Not only did Messi secure Miami's place in the FIFA Club World Cup 2025, but he also reminded everyone of why he's one of the greatest to ever play the game. The MLS was on notice; Messi had arrived, and he wasn't done yet.

Playoff Nightmare

In what was supposed to be a celebration of Messi's brilliance, Inter Miami's hopes of MLS Cup glory were dashed in a shocking upset by Atlanta United, who triumphed 3-2 in the opening round of the MLS Cup Playoffs at Chase Stadium. Miami, who had finished the regular season with a historic 74 points, earning the Supporters' Shield and the top spot in the league, found themselves eliminated by the ninth-seeded Atlanta, a team that barely made it into the playoffs. This 34-point gap, the largest in MLS postseason history, set the stage for a dramatic and unexpected clash.

Miami had entered the match with a 1-0 advantage from the first game of the series, but after a last-minute heartbreak in Atlanta and the inability to recover in this decisive home game, their postseason hopes were extinguished. The final blow came in a bizarre fashion. Inter Miami's center-back Tomás Avilés had gone down injured in the box in the middle of an Atlanta attack. Despite the apparent injury, Atlanta continued their relentless pursuit, and Pedro Amador's cross found Bartosz Slisz at the back post for the game-winning header.

For Messi, this was a crushing disappointment. With the MLS Cup aspirations surrounding Messi and his legendary roster, which had included former Barcelona teammates Luis Suárez, Sergio Busquets, and Jordi Alba, Miami was expected to cruise through the postseason. Instead, the team had faltered at the most critical stage. Despite Messi's involvement in setting up Miami's opening goal and his relentless play, including a vital assist in the first half, it hadn't been enough.

Miami had shown promise early in the match, with Messi orchestrating a goal in the 17th minute. He had set up a midfielder, who squared the ball for a rebound finish by another player. But two quick goals from Atlanta following poor clearances from Miami's defense had quickly evened the score. Then, another defensive lapse had seen Atlanta take a 2-1 lead, and despite constant pressure, Miami couldn't recover.

In the second half, even Messi's efforts hadn't been able to turn the tide. A crucial save by Atlanta's goalkeeper denied Suárez in stoppage time, and his performance in the series had ultimately proved to be the difference. Messi's stunning arrival in the U.S. had been supposed to bring a new era of success to MLS, but this early exit had left Miami fans, and Messi himself, with a sense of bitter disappointment.

Messi sparked hope in the 65th minute, collecting the ball at the edge of the box before linking up with Suárez. After a quick return pass, Messi dashed into the box, rising above defenders to head home a powerful goal. However, with Atlanta defending and countering, a bizarre sequence saw Aviles down in the box, and moments later, Miami's season ended in near silence.

Final Reflections

Lionel Messi opened up about his future in interviews, revealing that his time in football was nearing its end, with Inter Miami being his "last club." At 36 years old, Messi expressed his awareness of the limited time left in his illustrious career.

"There wasn't a lot of time left," he admitted, acknowledging that the end of his playing days was approaching. Despite the looming conclusion, Messi emphasized the importance of enjoying each moment: "I tried to enjoy it more because I was aware that there wasn't a lot of time left."

The World Cup win with Argentina in 2022 had brought a new perspective for Messi. "The fact we won the World Cup helped, it helped a lot, to see things in another way," he shared. For Messi, the triumph provided a sense of completion, as he had long aspired to win the tournament for his country, a feat he finally achieved. His perspective on the future shifted, allowing him to savor his remaining years in football. He spoke about cherishing the small details, like his time spent with teammates and the friendships formed along the way.

Messi also addressed the comparison between European and World Cup football, noting that while the Euro was important, "the best teams played in the World Cup." He highlighted Argentina's proud record and legacy as a three-time World Cup champion and underlined the significance of being part of such a prestigious tournament.

As for his participation in the 2026 World Cup, Messi was cautious. "I never gave much thought to records... but if it happened, if I was doing well, then perfect." He remained focused on living in the present, not chasing milestones for the sake of them. Messi's legacy, though, had already been cemented, and whether he played in 2026 or not, his impact on the game remained unparalleled.

Lionel Messi's decision to leave Barcelona was not easy, and it's clear that the departure still weighs on him. "I really wanted and was very excited about being able to return," Messi shared in an emotional reflection. However, his past experience at Barcelona, marked by a rushed and uncertain exit, made him hesitant to go through the same situation again.

Despite La Liga accepting Barcelona's plans, other financial and bureaucratic challenges loomed. "There were still many other things that needed to happen," Messi said, expressing his concern that things might fall apart again, just as they did when he was forced to leave for Paris Saint-Germain (PSG) in 2021. "I didn't want to go through all of that."

The challenges with Barcelona's financial situation were not lost on Messi, who felt that the club couldn't guarantee a smooth return. "I didn't want to be in the same situation again... waiting to see what would happen," he admitted. This uncertainty, paired with his family's support for his decision, ultimately led to him making the call to leave Barcelona for good.

Messi's family, too, had mixed feelings. "They were very excited about everything they heard," Messi said, acknowledging their desire to return to Barcelona, where they had all spent many happy years. But the reality of the situation and the uncertainty around his potential return made the decision difficult for all of them. Despite the challenges, Messi's family stood by him. "They are also happy about the new change, although also sad to leave," Messi noted.

His love for Barcelona was evident in his reflections, especially when he spoke about hearing his name sung at Camp Nou. "For me, it was beautiful," Messi said, appreciating the fans' continued affection even after his departure. It was a bittersweet feeling, knowing that he would have preferred to have had a proper farewell, as some of his former teammates had received. "I would have liked to leave that way, to have been able to say goodbye to the people well," he confessed.

As for his next step, Messi confirmed that a move to Saudi Arabia was never truly on his radar. Despite offers from Europe, his heart was set on returning to Barcelona—until reality set in. "After winning the World Cup and not being able to go to Barca, it was time to go to the American league," he explained.

His choice of Inter Miami came with a sense of peace, a fresh start in a league where he could "experience football in a different way." Messi remains driven, but his move to Miami signifies a change in how he approaches his career and personal life.

In the end, Messi's journey to Miami was not just about football. It was about family, closure, and a desire for a different experience. "With more peace of mind," Messi emphasized, signaling a new chapter in his illustrious career, free from the complexities and uncertainties that once surrounded him at Barcelona.

As Lionel Messi reflected on his journey—from the narrow streets of Rosario to the grandest stages of world football—he remained, at his core, the boy who simply loved to play. His career, marked by brilliance and perseverance, had transcended mere statistics or trophies; it had redefined the very essence of football itself. Even as he entered the twilight of his playing days, Messi's passion remained undiminished, his artistry still captivating millions. Whether wearing the colors of Barcelona, Argentina, or Inter Miami, his legacy was not just one of records broken but of dreams realized. And as long as there had been a ball at his feet, the world had continued to watch in awe, knowing that they had witnessed something truly extraordinary.

CAREER IN NUMBERS

1 - Trophies won with Inter Miami CF in the MLS after moving there in 2023.

1 - World Cup win with Argentina in 2022, adding to his accolades on the international stage.

2 - Ligue 1 titles won with PSG.

2 - Messi and Cristiano Ronaldo are the only players to have won more than three Ballon d'Or awards, with Messi now holding the record for the most wins.

4 - Champions League wins with Barcelona.

10 - La Liga titles with Barcelona.

16 - Age at which Messi made his Barcelona first-team debut.

47 - Seconds into his Argentina debut before he was sent off, against Hungary in 2005, aged 18, after coming on as a substitute.

52 - Career hat-tricks; 46 for Barcelona, 6 for Argentina.

67 - Messi's height in inches (5ft 7in).

91 - Goals scored in 2012, breaking the calendar-year record previously set by German Gerd Muller in 1972.

98 - Goals for PSG, showcasing his continued scoring prowess.

120 - Appearances for PSG from 2021 to 2023.

172 - Caps for Argentina, reflecting his continued involvement with the national team.

2008 - Olympic gold in Beijing remains Messi's only major honor with Argentina until the 2021 Copa América win.

36 - Trophies won with Barcelona, including league titles, cups, and international competitions.

614 - Goals scored for Barcelona, including a record 428 in La Liga.

701 - Appearances for Barcelona before his move to Paris Saint-

Germain (PSG) in 2021.

103 - Goals for Argentina, making him the nation's all-time leading scorer. This includes his notable contributions in multiple tournaments.

8 - Times he has won the Ballon d'Or, as the world's best player (in 2009, 2010, 2011, 2012, 2015, 2019, 2021, and 2023).